Thomas Carlyle, Joseph Reay Greene

Lectures on the History of Literature

Thomas Carlyle, Joseph Reay Greene

Lectures on the History of Literature

ISBN/EAN: 9783337058647

Printed in Europe, USA, Canada, Australia, Japan

Cover: Foto ©ninafisch / pixelio.de

More available books at **www.hansebooks.com**

LECTURES
ON
THE HISTORY OF LITERATURE
BY
THOMAS CARLYLE
1838

LECTURES

ON

HE HISTORY OF LITERATURE

DELIVERED BY

THOMAS CARLYLE

APRIL TO JULY 1838

NOW PRINTED FOR THE FIRST TIME

EDITED, WITH PREFACE AND NOTES

BY

PROFESSOR J. REAY GREENE

SECOND EDITION

LONDON
ELLIS AND ELVEY
1892

London:
Printed by STRANGEWAYS & SONS,
Tower Street, Cambridge Circus, W.C.

PREFACE.

The Lectures on Literature by Thomas Carlyle, published for the first time in the present volume, were delivered at 17 Edward Street, Portman Square, London, during the second quarter of the year 1838. Full reports of the twelve lectures, excepting the ninth, were taken by the late Mr. Thomas Chisholm Anstey, barrister-at-law and subsequently member of Parliament for Youghal. Mr. Anstey must have possessed considerable skill for the performance of his task. The reader will soon see for himself how unmistakeably many characteristics of Carlyle's style are here rendered.

Mr. Anstey had copies of these reports made by a few friends. Three such copies are known to exist. One, the property of the publishers, has been compared with a second copy kindly placed at their disposal by Professor Dowden, who has already noted samples of its contents in the opening pages of his interesting volume entitled—*Transcripts and Studies*. The two MSS., although the work of different hands, give concordant renderings throughout. The original MS. in Mr. Anstey's handwriting is now the property of the Asiatic Society, Bombay, who acquired it at his death.

To each lecture its date is here prefixed. As few changes as possible have been made in the way of correction. Slips concerning statements capable of verification and obviously due to momentary lapses of attention on the part of the reporter have in various cases been rectified. It must be remembered that Carlyle appears in our pages not as a writer but as a speaker. So, in estimating some doubtful locutions, it seemed best to follow the safe guide of analogy offered by the author's well-known Lectures on Heroes and Hero Worship, delivered in the same place, only two years later than the present course.

Why did not Carlyle issue these Lectures on Literature in his life-time? Doubtless he shrank from the slow labour of preparing for publication discourses which deal with topics demanding careful treatment while almost infinite in their extent and diversity. A prophet announcing high truths, he may not have felt himself so well fitted to do the work of a commentator. Fond as he was of needful repetitions, of variations on the same theme, after the manner of most impressive preachers and of some musicians, he had not the expansive suavity of exposition which is so charming in Malebranche. It may well have seemed to him an irksome business to spoil perhaps his own sentences, so effective when spoken, to weaken their force by critical interpolations. His natural impatience, his glowing productivity, urged him to other work. For in 1838 the genius of Carlyle may be said to have reached its highest and most fervid epoch.

Carlyle's *French Revolution*, acknowledged to be one of the best and most individual of his books, is not so much a history of that great chain of events as an apt selection of striking episodes, together with a running comment on other histories and on the lessons which revolutions should teach. The same may be said of the lectures before us. They do not constitute a manual. They are the more welcome on this account, for manuals of literature abound. They cannot rightly be blamed because of their omissions. They treat less of literature than of the causes of literature, its course and its significance.

We waive the opportunity here afforded us of adding one more to the multitude of essays on Carlyle as himself a power in literature. The reader perhaps will thank us. Carlyle was wont to say that in some golden age publishers and the public would see the wisdom of paying authors for what they do *not* write.

During the weeks that followed Carlyle's death and the appearance of the valuable biography by Mr. Froude the press teemed with notices passing judgment on our author and all things concerning him. Who now studies these notices? Have they any permanent value? Are they not like the æsthetic criticisms on Shakespeare, so little relished by the most devoted * of English Shakespeare-students? The good sense of many will turn from

* The late Mr. Halliwell-Phillips. See his *Memoranda on the Tragedy of Hamlet*, London, 1879.

reviews of Carlyle to Carlyle himself. He tells us in his first paragraph (page 2) that authors unlike heroes need no illumination from without; they are self-luminous. Carlyle's own brightness now makes him shine as a fixed star in our literary firmament. His radiance may be obscured; quenched it cannot be. His faults and foibles are manifest, yet is he esteemed in spite of them, and by too many because of them. His prejudices are vexatious, at least occasionally. So are those of De Quincey, at his best the best English prose-writer of this century. Amid all Carlyle's prejudices, amid all his denunciations of men and things to be condemned, we see him capable of hope; we feel he sympathises with his fellow-creatures. Beneath a mask of ferocity love beams from his countenance. Like Tasso's heroic prince—

> *Se'l miri fulminar fra l'arme auvolto.*
> *Marte lo stimi ; Amor se scopre il volto.*

No healthy man can doubt Carlyle's sincerity. We ought surely to greet with pleasure every combination of sincerity, ability, and amiability.

We courteously, therefore, invite the reader to enjoy the rich literary treat here set before him.

Our thanks are due to Professor Dowden for his kindness in placing his transcript of these Lectures at our disposal, and also to Mr. S. H. Hodivala of Bombay for information he has afforded us with respect to Mr. Anstey's original manuscript.

J. REAY GREENE.

Manor Lodge,
Tooting Graveney, London, S.W.
December 1891.

CONTENTS.

FIRST PERIOD.

LECTURE   PAGE

I.—OF LITERATURE IN GENERAL—LANGUAGE, TRADITION, RELIGIONS, RACES—THE GREEKS: THEIR CHARACTER IN HISTORY, THEIR FORTUNE, PERFORMANCE—MYTHOLOGIES—ORIGIN OF GODS .   1

II.—HOMER: THE HEROIC AGES—FROM ÆSCHYLUS TO SOCRATES—DECLINE OF THE GREEKS . .   16

III.—THE ROMANS: THEIR CHARACTER, THEIR FORTUNE, WHAT THEY DID—FROM VIRGIL TO TACITUS—END OF PAGANISM   36

SECOND PERIOD.

IV.—MIDDLE AGES—CHRISTIANITY; FAITH—INVENTIONS—PIOUS FOUNDATIONS—POPE HILDEBRAND—CRUSADES—TROUBADOURS—NIEBELUNGEN LIED   58

V.—DANTE—THE ITALIANS—CATHOLICISM—PURGATORY   79

VI.—THE SPANIARDS—CHIVALRY—GREATNESS OF THE SPANISH NATION—CERVANTES, HIS LIFE, HIS BOOK—LOPE—CALDERON—PROTESTANTISM AND THE DUTCH WAR   97

LECTURE PAGE

VII.—THE GERMANS—WHAT THEY HAVE DONE—RE-
FORMATION—LUTHER—ULRICH VON HUTTEN—
ERASMUS 118

VIII.—THE ENGLISH: THEIR ORIGIN, THEIR WORK
AND DESTINY—ELIZABETHAN ERA—SHAKE-
SPEARE—JOHN KNOX—MILTON—BEGINNING OF
SCEPTICISM 139

THIRD PERIOD.

IX.—VOLTAIRE—THE FRENCH—SCEPTICISM—FROM
RABELAIS TO ROUSSEAU.

Of this Lecture no record exists.

X.—EIGHTEENTH CENTURY IN ENGLAND—WHIT-
FIELD—SWIFT—STERNE—JOHNSON—HUME . 161

XI.—CONSUMMATION OF SCEPTICISM—WERTHERISM
—THE FRENCH REVOLUTION 178

FOURTH PERIOD.

XII.—OF MODERN GERMAN LITERATURE—GOETHE AND
HIS WORKS 197

LECTURES

ON

THE HISTORY OF LITERATURE.

LECTURE I.

April 27th.

FIRST PERIOD.

OF LITERATURE IN GENERAL—LANGUAGE, TRADITION, RELIGIONS, RACES — THE GREEKS: THEIR CHARACTER IN HISTORY, THEIR FORTUNE, PERFORMANCE—MYTHOLOGIES—ORIGIN OF GODS.

It must surely be an interesting occupation to follow the stream of mind from the periods at which the first great spirits of our western world wrote and flourished, down to these times. He who would pursue the investigation, however, must commence by inquiring what it was these men *thought* before he inquires what they *did*; for, after all, these were solely remarkable for mind, thought, opinion—opinion which clothed itself in action, and their opinions have survived in their books. A book affords matter for deep meditation. Upon their shelves books seem queer, insignificant things, but in reality there is nothing so important as a book is. It stirs up the minds of men long after the author has sunk into the grave, and continues to exert its corresponding influence for ages. Authors unlike heroes, therefore, do not need to be illuminated by others; they are of themselves luminous. The thought that was produced to-day, the pamphlet that was published to-day, are only, as it were, reprints of thoughts that have circulated ever since the world began. And we are interested in its history, for the thought is alive with us, and it lives when we are dead.

There is a very great difficulty in reducing this generation of thought to a perfect theory, as indeed there is with everything else, except, perhaps, the stars only, and even they are not reduced to theory; not perfectly, at least, for, although the solar system is quite established as such, it seems doubtful whether it does not in its turn revolve round other solar systems, and so any theory is, in fact, only imperfect. This phenomenon, therefore, is not to be theorised on; something, however, is necessary to be done in order to familiarise ourselves with it. We shall see this great stream of thought, bearing with it its strange phenomenon of literary productions, divide itself into regular periods; and we will commence with the facts to be discovered in the history of the Greeks.

The Greek records go back as far as 1800 years before our era, that is, 3600 years or so from the present time. But they cannot be considered as authentic at that antiquity. When we ask the question, Who were the first inhabitants of Greece? or, Were they the same as that modern nation by some called Græci, by others, Hellenes, and by us, Greeks? we can derive no clear account from any source. They seem to have been called Pelasgi. There is a controversy whether these Hellenes were Pelasgi, or new settlers from the East. They were probably Pelasgi, with whom thought had begun to operate a progress in science and civilisation; and these gave their local name Hellenes to the rest, just as was the case with the Angles and the Saxons. We have no good history of Greece. This is not at all remarkable. Greek transactions had never anything alive; no result for us; they were dead entirely. The only points which serve to guide us are a few ruined towns, a few masses of stone, and some broken statuary. In this point of view we can trace three epochs, not more, after the introduction of civilised arts into the country, and the formation of societies.

1. The first is the siege of Troy, which happened in the twelfth century B.C., and was instituted by the Achaioi, as they were then called, or Hellenes. It seems that there is evidence that they were at that time the same as Pelasgi. The siege, as is well known, is said to have been occasioned by Paris carrying off a Greek girl, the famous Helen, wife of Menelaus. Herodotus speaks of many such cases—Io, for example, and Europa. He remarks very properly that it is really very foolish to go to war

for such a reason, as the lady is always sure to be as much to blame herself as her seducer. Whatever, however, was the reason, this was the first confederate act of the Hellenes in their capacity of an European people. The town was taken and destroyed. The immediate cause which was assigned may not have been true; but, by the European Pelasgi, it seems to have been chiefly ascribed to their superiority over Asia; this was the constant *gesta* of the narrative. The event is also important in giving rise to the first valuable work of antiquity after the Bible, the Homeric Poems, comprising the Iliad and the Odyssey.

Of the date of 600 years later we have the marble chronicles now preserved in the University of Oxford, which an Earl of Arundel brought out of the East in the reign of James I., and which arrived here about the year 1627. They suffered much during the civil wars, and lay mutilated a long time in the garden of Arundel House at Lambeth. One of them even was built up by the gardener into the garden wall. Among the most remarkable was the marble called the Chronicle of Paros, containing a record of some very memorable events. It is uncertain why it was so called. Near the spot where it was found a new colony was founded 264 B.C., and, as it was the custom to erect these records on such occasions, it is presumed that the above was the date of its erection. Herodotus lived in the fifth century B.C., but it was *clean* after that.

2. The second epoch was that of the Persian invasion. Greece had **then** to support itself against the innumerable hosts of the East poured out against her. This is the great *gesta* of Herodotus' history : the gallant resistance of a handful of Greeks, for they were far from being unanimous. Their fate trembled in the iron scale of destiny for a while. At Thermopylæ Leonidas repelled the Persians during three days; on the fourth, circumvented by treachery, he was overwhelmed with numbers, and he and his troops were cut **to** pieces; not a man survived, they wouldn't give up the place. One fancies that *that* monument must have had a wonderful effect for ages after; the marble lion with the inscription, 'O stranger! tell the Lacedæmonians that we lie here according to the laws.' They were ordered to remain, not to quit the post, and there they lay for ever. But Europe was ever afterwards superior to Persia. The Grecian societies **soon afterwards divided more and** more until they became a kind of federal republic, united only by common habits, and mainly by their religion. It is a pity that during this time we have but little information as to the influence produced upon them by the aspect of their beautiful country, its lofty mountains and fertile valleys, the gigantic trees which clothed the summits and sides of their craggy precipices, and all too beautifully set off by the bright sky which was shining upon them; as well as the means by which all this was rendered serviceable to them in the ways of daily life. It is only battles

that are marked by historians, but subjects like these are rarely noticed.

They spread themselves abroad in new colonies at this time, but there were already Greek colonies even before that. They had built towns and cities, which still exist on the south coast of Italy, or Magna Græcia as it is generally called. Indeed, I am told that the people in the mountains still speak a kind of Greek up in the Abruzzi. They built Marseilles in France before the Persian invasion. Herodotus records the Phocean emigration. They wandered a long time before they could find a convenient spot for their new settlement; but, to extinguish all hope of return, their leader took a red-hot ball of iron and plunged it into the sea, and called the gods to witness that he and his followers would never return to Phocea until that ball of iron should float upon the surface. They afterwards landed at Marseilles, and founded a flourishing republic there.

3. The third great epoch, like the other two, has also reference to the East. It was the flower time of Greece—her history is as that of a tree from its sapling state to its decline; and at this period she developed an efflorescence of genius such as no other country ever beheld, but it speedily ended in the shedding of her flowers and in her own decay. From that time she has continued to fall, and Greece has never again been such as she then was. About the year 330 B.C. she was subjected to the king of a foreign state, Macedon. Alexander the

Great found little trouble in ruling Greece, enfeebled already by the Peloponnesian war, a war of which one cannot see the reason, except that each contending party seems to have striven merely for its own gain, while their country stood by to see which side of the collision was to grind it down. Philip of Macedon, a strong, active man, had already got it united under him. Under Alexander occurred the memorable invasion of Persia, when Greece exploded itself on Asia. He carried his arms to the banks of the Indus, founded kingdoms, and left them to his followers; insomuch that they continued a remarkable set of people till long afterwards. Nor was it till 1453 A.D. that they were finally conquered in Constantinople.

This, then, is the history of Greece. The siege of Troy, the first epoch, took place in the year 1184 B.C. The Battle of Marathon, 490 B.C.; and 160 years later came the invasion of Persia. Europe was henceforth to develop herself on an independent footing, and it had been so ordered that Greece was to begin that. As to their peculiar physiognomy among nations, they were in one respect an extremely interesting people; but, in another, unamiable and weak entirely. It has been somewhere remarked by persons learned in the speculation on what is called the doctrine of races, that the Pelasgi were of Celtic descent. However this may be, it is certain that there is a remarkable similarity in character of the French to these Greeks. Their first feature was what we may call the central feature of all others existing, *vehemence*, not exactly *strength*, for there was no permanent coherence in it as in strength, but a sort of fiery impetuosity, a vehemence never anywhere so remarkable as among the Greeks, except among the French. And there are instances of this both in its good and bad point of view. As to the bad, there is the instance mentioned by Thucydides of the sedition in Corcyra, which really does read like a chapter out of the French Revolution, in which the actors seem to be quite regardless of any moment but that which was at hand. Here, too, the lower classes were at war upon the higher or aristocrats, as the French would have called them. They suspected a design on the part of the aristocracy to carry them as slaves off to Athens, and on their side it ended in the aristocracy being all shut up in prison; man after man they were brought out of the prison, and then with stabs and pikes they were massacred one after another (this is all told by Thucydides) until those within the prison, finding what was going on, would not come out when summoned, whereupon the mob fired arrows upon them until they were all destroyed. In short, the whole scene recalls to the reader the events of September 1792.

Another instance, but more justifiable, was the following:—When Xerxes first invaded Greece, an Athenian, Lycidas, proposed to the citizens to surrender the city, as it was impossible to make head against the Persians. The Athenians assembled, jostled, struck, and trampled upon him till he died. The women of the place, hearing this, went to his house, attacked his wife and children, and stabbed them to death. There was nothing ever like this behaviour or that at Corcyra known in other countries in ancient times; as among the Romans, for example, during their dominant period.

But connected with all this savageness there was an extraordinary delicacy of taste and genius in them. They had a prompt dexterity in seizing the true relations of objects, a beautiful and quick sense in perceiving the places in which the things lay all round the world which they had to work with, and which, without being entirely admirable, was in their own internal province highly useful. So the French, with their undeniable barrenness of genius, have yet in a remarkable manner the faculty of expressing themselves with precision and elegance to so singular a degree that no ideas or inventions can possibly become popularised till they are presented to the world by means of the French language.

And this is true of history, and of all things now in the world, of all philosophy, and of everything else; but in poetry, philosophy, and all things, the Greek *genius* displays itself with as curious a felicity as the French does in frivolous exercises. Singing or music was the central principle of the Greeks, not a subordinate one, and they were right. What is not musical is rough and hard, and cannot be harmonised. Harmony is the essence of art and science. The mind moulds to itself the clay, and makes it what it will. The Pelasgic architecture, which still subsists in its huge walls of stone, formed of immense boulders piled one upon another, presents, I am told, now at the distance of 3000 years the evidence of most magnificent symmetry and an eye to what is beautiful. Their poems are equally admirable. Their statuary comprises still the highest things that we have to show for ourselves in that art. Phidias, for example, **had the same spirit of harmony**, and the matter of his art was obedient to him. His Jupiter of Elis must have been a memorable work, it seems to me. Phidias superintended the building of *that thing*, the Parthenon, and, perhaps, the Elgin marbles received his corrections. When he projected, however, his Jupiter of Elis his ideas were so confused and bewildered as to give him great unrest, and he wandered about perplexed that the shape he wished would not disclose itself. But one night, after struggling in pain with his thoughts as usual, and meditating on his design, in a dream he saw a group of Grecian maidens approach with pails of water on their heads, who began a song in praise of Jupiter. At that moment the sun of poetry stared upon him and set free the image which he sought for, and it crystallised as it were out of his mind into marble, and became as symmetry itself. This spirit of **harmony** operated directly in him, informing all parts of his mind, thence transferring itself into statuary, and seen with **the eye and filling the hearts of all people**.

I shall now call your attention to the opinions entertained by the Greeks on all things that concerned this world, or what we call their religion. Polytheism seems at first sight an inextricable mass of confusions and delusions; but there was, no doubt, some meaning in it for the people. It may be explained in one of two ways. The first is, that the fable was only an allegory to explain the various relations of natural facts (of spiritual facts and material), and much learning has been expended on this theory. Bacon himself wrote upon it in his treatise 'De Sapientia Veterum.'

But I think there is little or nothing to be made out of that. To tell fabulous stories of that kind does not seem a natural process in the diffusion of science. No man in such a case would have sat down to make out something which all the while he knew to be a lie; no serious man would do it. The second opinion is, that their gods were simply their kings and heroes, whom they afterwards deified. There is more probability in this theory, which is called Euhemerism. Man is always venerable to man. Great men are sure to attract worship or reverence in all ages, and in ancient times it is not wonderful that sometimes they were accounted as gods; for the most imaginative of us can scarcely conceive the feelings with which the earliest of the human species looked abroad on the world around them. At first, doubtless, they regarded nothing but the gratification of their wants, as, in fact, wild people do yet; but the man would soon begin to ask himself whence he was, what were his flesh and blood, what he himself was, who was not here a short time ago, who will not be here much longer, but still existing a conscious individual in this immense universe. The theories so formed would be extremely extravagant, and little would suffice to shape the system into Polytheism; for it is really, in my opinion, a blasphemy against human nature to attribute the whole of the system to quackery and falsehood.

Divination, for instance, was the great nucleus round which Polytheism formed itself—the constituted *core* of the whole matter. All people, private men as well as states, used to consult the oracle of Dodona or Delphi (which eventually became the most celebrated of all) on all the concerns of life. Modern travellers have discovered in those places pipes and other secret contrivances, from which they have concluded that these oracles were constituted on a principle of falsehood and delusion. Cicero, too, said that he was certain two augurs could not meet without laughing, and he was likely to know, for he had once been an augur himself. But I confess that on reading Herodotus there appears to me to have been very little quackery about it. I can quite readily fancy that there was a great deal of reason in the oracle. The seat of that at Dodona was a deep, dark chasm, into which the diviner entered when he sought the Deity. If he was a man of devout frame of mind he must surely have then been in the best state of feeling for foreseeing the future, and giving advice to others. No matter how this was carried on, by divination or otherwise, so long as the individual suffered himself to be rapt in union with a higher being. I like to believe better of Greece than that she was completely at the mercy of fraud and falsehood in these matters. So before the Battle of Marathon, an Athenian, Philippides, set off to Lacedæmon for supplies; he ran nearly the whole way. As he was travelling among the mountains near Tegea he heard the God Pan calling out to him, 'Philippides, why do the Athenians neglect me?' He obtained the succours demanded, and returned to Athens to find his citizens victorious, and on his relating the above circumstance a temple was erected to Pan, and his worship attended to. Now, when I consider the frame of mind he must have been in, I have no doubt that he really heard in his own mind that voice of the God of Nature upon the wild mountain-side, and that this was not done by quackery or falsehood at all. To this system there was a deeper basis than the mere plan of gods and goddesses, such as Jupiter, Apollo, Minerva, &c. Subordinate functions only were assigned them. But, independently of their idolatry, they discovered that truth, which is in every man's heart, and to which no thinking man can refuse his assent. They recognised a destiny, a great dumb black power, ruling during time, which knew nobody for its master, and in its decrees was as inflexible as adamant, and every one knew that it was there.

It was sometimes called Μοῖρα, or 'allotment,' 'part,' and sometimes 'the Unchangeable.'

Their gods were not always mentioned with reverence. There is a strange document on the point, the Prometheus of Æschylus. Æschylus wrote three plays of Prometheus, but only one has survived to our times. Prometheus had introduced fire into the world, and he was punished for that. His design was to make our race a little less wretched than it was. Personally he seems to be a taciturn sort of man, but what he does speak seems like a thunderbolt against Jupiter. These miserable men were wandering about in ignorance of the arts of life, and he taught them to them. It was right in him to do it! Jupiter may launch his thunderbolts, and do what he will with him. A time is coming; he awaits his time! Jupiter can hurl him to Tartarus, his time is coming too; he must come down; it is all written in the book of Destiny.

This curious document really indicates the primeval qualities of man. So Herodotus, who was a clear-headed, candid man, tells us that a Scythian nation, the Getæ, when it thundered, or the sky was long clouded, used to shoot arrows in the air against the god, and defied him, and were excessively angry with him. Another people, whom he mentions with less credibility, made war on the south wind; probably it had blown on them till it made them quite desperate. They marched against it into the desert, but were never heard of again.

These are things alien to our ways of thinking, but they may serve to illustrate Greek life.

I must here conclude my remarks on the character of the Greeks. In my next lecture I shall take a survey of the history of their literature from Homer down to Socrates.

LECTURE II.

May 4th.

FIRST PERIOD—*continued*.

HOMER: THE HEROIC AGES — FROM ÆSCHYLUS TO SOCRATES — DECLINE OF THE GREEKS.

WE must now take a survey of Greek literature, although our time does not afford us much scope for diverging, as we must do, over a space of more than 500 years.

The first works which we shall notice are the poems of Homer. These treat of that event which, as I mentioned in my last lecture, constitutes the first great epoch of Grecian History, the Siege of Troy. The Iliad, or Song of Ilion, consists of a series of what I call ballad delineations of the various occurrences which took place then, rather than of a narrative of the event itself; for it begins in the middle of it, and, I might say, ends in the middle of it. The Odyssey relates the adventures and voyages of Odysseus or Ulysses on his return from Troy. Their age, as indicated by the Arundel Marbles, and still more by Herodotus, was 800 years B.C. At all events, that was the age of **the Iliad**, or perhaps 900. Johannes von Müller says of them that they are the oldest books of importance after the Bible. There are none older even among the Chinese, for, in spite of what has been said about their works, there is no evidence that any of them are any older than the poems of Homer. Some there are about the same age, but very insignificant, such as romances or chronicles. Who this Homer was, or who was the real author of these poems, is almost unknown to us. There is, indeed, a bust of Homer in the museum presented by the Earl of Arundell, and there are one or two other busts of him elsewhere; but we have not the slightest evidence for believing that either of them is a portrait. It is not certain whether his poems were the work of one or many writers. There is a tradition, indeed, of a singer, Όμηρος, a beggar and blind man, to whom they have been attributed; and the belief in his identity was common till 1780, when in Germany, Wolff, who had been employed to write a Prolegomena of a Glasgow edition of Homer, for the first time started an opinion which has much startled and confused the learned, that there was no such man as Homer, and that the Iliad had occupied a century or more in its composition, and that it was the work of various itinerant singers or poets who came to seek a welcome in the courts of different Grecian princes; for there were at that time thousands of songs about Troy circulated throughout Greece. It was 300 years after their date when the first edition of Homer's poems was published by the sons of Pisistratus, Hippias and Hipparchus. This was the first. Lycurgus, indeed, is said by Plutarch to have already made a collection of them; but what he says is extremely vague and unsupported. The next edition was collected by Alexander the Great, which, with some alterations, is our present edition. There appears to me to be a great improbability that any one would compose an epic except in writing. Other poems were intended for recital, but this was too long to be repeated in one sitting; and, on the other hand, they would not have been written if, as was the case, there were then no readers. It is also an established fact that Homer could not write. He talks himself of messages passing from one chief to another, when it is clear from his own expressions that they made use, not of letters at all, but of some kind of hieroglyphics. Indeed, the only argument in favour of Homer being the real author is derived from the common opinion on the point and from the unity of the poem, of which it was once said that it was as unlikely that it **should** be owing to an accidental concurrence of distinct writers as that, by an accidental arrangement of the types, it should have printed itself. But I began myself some time ago to read the Iliad, which I **had not** looked at since I left school, and I must confess that from reading alone **I became completely** convinced that it was not the work of one man. Knight himself, one of the warmest adherents of the other side, conceded that the Odyssey was written by a different hand, and that the Iliad, as we have it, has been much altered by transcribers. In short, he is not at all strong for his own side. But by far the strongest consideration for the opinion is produced by reading the poem itself. As to its unity, I confess that it seems to me that one may cut out two or three books without making any alteration in its unity. Its value does not consist in an excellent sustaining of characters. There is not at all the sort of style in which Shakespeare draws his characters; there is simply the cunning man; the great-headed, coarse, stupid man; the proud man; but there is nothing so remarkable but that any one else could have drawn the same characters for the purpose of piecing them into the Iliad. We all know the old Italian comedy: their Harlequin, Doctor, and Columbine. There are almost similar things in the characters in the Iliad. Hence, if we may compare great things with small, we have an analogous case in this country's literature. We have collections of songs about Robin Hood, a character who lived as an outlaw in Sherwood Forest, and was particularly famous in Nottinghamshire and the north of England. In the fourteenth century innumerable ballads respecting him were current in this country, and especially in the north, about his disputes with sheriffs, and great quantities of adventures of all sorts, which were sung, quite in an independent character, by fiddlers and old blind men. It is only fifty years since a bookseller of York published those ballads in an uniform collection; cut out parts here and put in other parts there, and rendered the whole to as consistent a poem as the Iliad. Now, contrasting the melodious Greek mind with the not very melodious English mind, the cithara with the fiddle (between which, by the way there is strong resemblance), and having in remembrance that those of the one class were sung in alehouses, while the others were sung in kings' houses, it really appears that Robin Hood ballads have received the very same arrangement as that which in other times produced 'the Tale of Troy divine.'

With Johannes von Müller, I should say that the character of Homer's poems is the best among all poems. For, in the first place, they are the delineation of something more ancient than themselves and more simple, and therefore more interesting as being the impressions of a primeval mind, the proceedings of a set of men our spiritual progenitors. The first things of importance in the world's history are mentioned there. Secondly, they possess qualities of the highest character of whatever age or country. The Greek genius never exceeded what was done by the authors of those poems which are known as the writings of Homer. Those qualities may be reduced to these two heads:

First. Homer does not seem to believe his story to be a fiction; he has no doubt of its truth. Now, if we only consider what a thing it is *to believe*, we shall see that it must have been an immense circumstance in favour of Homer. I do not mean to say that Homer could have sworn to the truth of his poems before a jury—far from it; but that he repeated what had survived in tradition and records, and expected his readers to believe them as he did. With regard to that thing which we call machinery, such as gods, visions, and the like, I must recall to your minds what I said in my last lecture respecting the belief which the Greeks had in their deities. It is of no moment to our question that these stories were altogether false, but Homer believed them to be true. Throughout the whole of Grecian history we find that any remarkable man, any man to whom anything mysterious attached, was regarded as of the supernatural. Their experience was narrow, and men's hearts opened to the marvellous, not being yet shut up by scepticism. This disposition was favourable to the plastic nature of Rumour, and Rumour, in fact, became afterwards one of the gods, and temples were raised to it. Thus Pindar mentions that Ποσειδῶν (Neptune) appeared on one occasion at the Nemæan games. Here it is conceivable that if some aged individual of venerable mien and few words had, in fact, come thither, his appearance would have attracted attention; people would have come to gaze upon him, and conjecture would have been busy. It would be natural that a succeeding generation should actually report that a god appeared upon the earth. Therefore I am convinced that Homer believed his narratives to be strictly true.

Secondly. The poem of the Iliad was actually intended to be sung. It sings itself; not only the cadence, but the whole thought of the poem sings itself, as it were: there is a serious recitative in the whole matter. Now, if we take these two things and add them together, the combination makes up the essence of the best poem that can be written. In that pitch of enthusiasm in which the whole was conceived the very words sing. In the strong high emotion the very tones of the voice grow musical. Homer throws in the expletives of some short sentences. With these two qualities, music and belief, he places his mind in a most beautiful brotherhood, in a sincere contact with his own characters; there are no reticences. He allows himself to expand with most touching loveliness, and occasionally it may be with an awkwardness that carries its own apology, upon all the matters which come in view of the subject of his work, and thus he affords the most decisive impression of the truly poetic nature of his genius.

We can see it in his very language, his phraseology, and the most minute details of his work. Let us take, for instance, the epithets which he applies to the objects of nature: 'the Divine sea' (the beauty of that Divine sea was deep in the mind of Homer), 'the dark coloured sea;' or to the king's houses which he admired, 'the high wainscotted house,' 'the sounding house.' For a very touching instance, let us see Agamemnon when he swears, not merely by the gods, but by rivers and all objects, stars, &c., and calls on them to witness his oath. He does not say what they *are*, but he feels that he himself is a mysterious existence, standing by the side of them, mysterious existences!

There is more of character in his second poem, supposed to have been written a century later than the Iliad; it treats of a higher state of civilisation. There is an evident alteration, too, in the theology. In the first poem Pallas is represented as mixing in fights. In the second poem she does not fight at all, but is Minerva, or rather Athena, the Goddess of Wisdom. From the superior unity of it as a poem, it is impossible that it could have been written by many different people. It makes a deeper impression on one than the Iliad, though the genius of it is not greater, perhaps not so great. The heroes are different. Ulysses does not make much figure in the Iliad; he is merely drawn an adroit, shifty, cunning man; but in the Odyssey he becomes of a tragic significance. He is not there the man of cunning and stratagem, but the '*much enduring*,' a most endearing epithet! We have a touching account of all his experiences in misfortune. He proves himself in the later poem more thoughtful of those who have perished. What, for example, can be more lovely than the scene when, after escaping the man-devouring Læstrygonians, the snares of Circe, and other perils, he comes to the end of the Old World, the pillars of Hercules, to consult Tiresias the prophet, and after performing different oblations among the surrounding shades, he sees the shade of his mother Anticlea, and poor Ulysses stands there, and there is his mother, a pale, ineffectual shade, and he strives to clasp her in his arms, and he finds nothing but air! In all nations we read and hear of such feelings as that; we go for them into the heart of human nature. The same sentiment, for instance, we meet with in those beautiful lines of the 'Queen's Marys.' That, too, is a beautiful burst of anger where Ulysses, concealed in his own palace, beholds the shameful waste, the wild revel and riot of his wife's unworthy suitors. He is disguised as a beggar, and is known to no one until his old nurse discovers him by a scar in his leg, which she observes while washing his feet. The suitors treated him with insult, and flung bones and all sorts of things at him. Lastly, they tried to bend Ulysses' bow; but the old bow was too strong for them. The old beggar begged hard for a trial; he took the bow, and with a fiery kindness and love for his old friend, examined it a long time without saying a word, to see if it were in the state in which he left it. Then he shook his rags, and, as Homer says, 'he strode mightily across the threshold,' and began to address the suitors. 'Ye dogs,' he says, 'ye thought that I should never return again from Troy, and ye gave way to your wickedness, unmindful of gods above and men below; but now your time is come. The extreme limits of death await you.' Then his arrows fell thick among them, and I believe there was quick work made with the suitors on that occasion. Numbers of traits like these have been collected by Goethe. There is an immense number of similes in Homer. Sometimes their simplicity makes us smile; but there is great kindness and veneration in the smile. Thus, where he compares Ajax to an ass, Homer does not mean anything like insult in the comparison; but he means to compare him, surrounded as he is by an overwhelming force of Trojans, to an ass getting into a field of corn, while all the boys of the neighbourhood are endeavouring by blows and shouts to drive him away; but the slow ass, unheeding them, crops away at the quick-growing corn, and will not leave off till he has had his fill. So it is with Ajax and the Trojans. There is a beautiful formula which he always uses when he describes death. 'He thumped down falling, and his arms jingled about him.' Now, trivial as this expression may at first appear, it does convey a deep sight and feeling of that phenomenon. The fall, as it were, of a sack of clay, and the jingle of armour, the last sound he was ever to make throughout time, who a minute or two before was alive and vigorous, and now falls a heavy dead mass!

But we must quit Homer. There is one thing, however, which I ought to mention about Ulysses, that he is the very model of the type Greek, a perfect image of the Greek genius, a shifty, nimble, active man, involved in difficulties, but every now and then bobbing up out of darkness and confusion, victorious and intact

But I must quit this discussion about Homer, and I regret it much. I must omit altogether the insight into heroic times which he affords us: that farmer-grazier life; the pillars of their halls covered with smoke, as he describes them; the stable-yard at the principal portal to those king's houses, high sounding houses, which he so much admires, piled up with sweepings of the stables, and other curious delineations of manners; I must leave all that. Homer already betokens a high state of civilisation; in fact, by tradition, and still more by express records, we learn that the Greek genius had been then for 1000 years working. As Horace says of their warriors, that 'there were many brave men before Agamemnon,' we may say of their authors, that there were many beautiful and musical minds before Homer, of whom we have no account. The language, for example, was the best dialect, the most complete language that was ever spoken. If, from its precision and excellence, the French language is best adapted to chat and to courts and compliments, the Greek was no less suited to every kind of composition, down to the pointed epigram. Their theology, too; their polity, both of war and peace, presupposes a civilisation of 1000 years or longer before Homer. After Homer, with the exception of some minstrels, whom I like to fancy kindred to the Troubadours (on which point I shall say more when I come to the Troubadours), we have nothing in the way of literature for 400 or 500 years. It was an age of war, convulsions, and migrations, about the

Heraclidæ and others. Greece expanded itself in colonisation, however, and other enterprises of an important character. The Greek mind at this epoch was rather philosophical than poetical. Pythagoras and the Seven Wise Men were of this time.

What we have of these philosophers is very vague. One man speculated that the world was made out of fire; another attributed it to the operation of water. There is something very enigmatic about Pythagoras, the greatest man among them. Some of his precepts which are preserved, our want of information makes us consider entirely absurd and ridiculous.

We cannot, for instance, understand the reason for his precept, abstain from beans — 'fabâ abstine.' What will immortalise Pythagoras is his discovery of the square of the hypothenuse. It seems that he may rather be said not to have invented it, but to have imported it, for I understand the Hindoos and other people of the East have long known it. It was a discovery, however, which in an advancing state of science could not remain unguessed. But a great part of the wisdom of our world was due to Pythagoras, who acquired it in travelling over the world for information. It may have been talent, and it may not be easy to indicate what precisely we owe to him; but it was not lost while men were to be found to work and improve on what he had left them. We may observe the like of many men. The print, then, which Pythagoras has left of his genius is the forty-seventh proposition of Euclid. There is also another one we owe to the Greeks. Archimedes discovered that the circumference of the sphere is three times as great as a line drawn through the centre from the opposite points of the circle which goes round it.

Passing from philosophy to history, we come to a remarkable man, Herodotus. He was not exactly the next writer in order of time, as Æschylus preceded him by a few years. His history is divided by his admiring editors into nine books, which they named after the Nine Muses, or rather the division was made by him, while the designation and admiration were theirs. He was a native of Halicarnassus, and being early engaged in some of the troubles of that place, he was obliged to leave it, and set out on his travels. He attentively studied the histories of the various countries he visited, from Egypt to the Black Sea, and he put down everything he learned in writing; for there were no books then, and, as he mentions, all the chronicles of importance were inscribed on tablets of brass. At the age of thirty-nine he returned to Greece, and he read his work at the Olympic Games, where it excited intense admiration. It is, properly speaking, an encyclopedia of the various nations, and it displays in a striking manner the innate spirit of harmony that was in the Greeks. It begins with Crœsus, king of Lydia. Upon some hint or other, it suddenly goes off into a digression on the Persians, and then, apropos of something else, we have a disquisition on the Egyptians, and so on. At first we feel somewhat impatient of being thus carried away at the 'sweet will' of the author; but we soon find it to be the result of an instinctive spirit of harmony, and we see all these various branches of the tale come pouring down at last in the invasion of Greece by the Persians. It is that spirit of order which has constituted him the prose poet of his country. It is curious to see the world he made for himself. There is, in general, not a more veracious man, a more intelligent man, than Herodotus. We see, as in a mirror, that what he writes from his own observation is quite true. But when he does not profess to know the truth of his narratives, it is curious to see the sort of Arabian Tales which he collects together—of the nation of one-eyed men, of the Female Republic, the Amazons, of the people who live under an air always black with feathers, the Cimmerians; yet even here the man's natural shrewdness is often evinced, as when he conjectures that the feathers may have been only falling snow-flakes; and thus dying away gradually from authentic history into the fabulous. He was a good-natured man, not at all against the Persians; but still there is an emphasis in the way he reports things, where the war with Persia is concerned, and in the speeches which he attributes to his characters, that shows the Greek feeling he had in him. He mentions with very little reproof the Lacedæmonian irregularity; how the people took the Persian heralds who came to demand earth and water in token of submission, and flung them into a deep well, and told them that they would find both there in plenty. His account is the only one we have of that war. It is mainly through him that we become acquainted with Themistocles, that model of the type Greek in prose as Ulysses was in song. He lived, too, in that which I have called the *Flower Period of Greece*, fifty years after the Persian invasion, or 445 B.C., which, counting in the whole 100 years, was the most brilliant period of Grecian history. Themistocles was certainly one of the greatest men in the world. Had it not been for him, the Persians would have unquestionably conquered Greece. It is curious to observe the vacillations of the Greeks at this period. The Greeks wished to run and not to fight at all. Even after Leonidas had so gallantly perished, Themistocles had great difficulty in persuading them not to take to flight in their ships; if once they went to sea, **he** said, all was lost. And then his reply to Eurybiades, which has been by some censured, appears to me to have been one of the grandest ever made by man. Eurybiades, in the heat of **dispute**, shook his staff in a menacing manner at him. 'Strike, but hear,' was the only return he made. To have drawn forth the sword by his side, and to have smote him dead for such an insult, would have been no more than natural; but any one could have done that. A poor drayman in a pothouse might have done it; but to forbear, to waive his own redress in order to extinguish resentments, and keep the troops united for his country's sake, this appears to me truly great! Like Ulysses, he displayed an uncommon degree of dexterity on occasions. For instance, when he was chased out of Greece he betook himself to his worst enemy, the king of the Persians, whose armies he had destroyed, and who had offered a price for his head, but who now had the magnanimity to do him no wrong. At his first audience the king asked him what he thought of Greece. Themistocles, who felt that he knew nothing at all that he could answer to such a question, replied adroitly 'that speech was like a Persian carpet rolled up, which was full of beautiful colours and images, but which required to be unrolled and spread out before the colours or the figures would be seen and appreciated. He therefore requested time to acquire a sufficient knowledge of the Persian tongue to be able to afford the king the information he sought in one single view, and not in a detached, disjointed fashion.' The answer satisfied the king.

Contemporary with Themistocles, and a little prior to Herodotus, Greek tragedy began. Æschylus I define to have been a *truly gigantic man* (I mean by this much more than the mere trivial figure of elocution usually expressed by the word gigantic), one of the largest characters ever known, and all whose movements are clumsy and huge, like those of a son of Anak. In short, his character is just that of Prometheus himself as he has described him. I know no more pleasant thing than to study Æschylus. You fancy that you hear the old dumb rocks speaking to you of all things they had been thinking of since the world began, in their wild, savage utterances. His Agamemnon opens finely with the watchman on the top of a high tower, where he has been waiting a year, day and night, for the expected telegraph of the success of his countrymen. All at once, while he is yet speaking, the fire begins blazing. It is a very grand scene; Clytemnestra afterwards describes most graphically that signal fire, consuming the dry heath on Mount Ida, then prancing over the billows of the ocean, reflected from mountain top to mountain top, and lastly coming to Salamis. Æschylus had himself borne arms, and he must have been a terrible fright, quite a Nemæan lion; and one says to oneself, when one reads his descriptions, 'Heaven help the Persians who had to deal with Æschylus.' It is said that when composing he had on a look of the greatest fierceness. He has been accused of bombast. From his obscurity he is often exceedingly difficult; but bombast is not the word at all. His words come up from the great volcano of his heart, and often he has no voice for it, and it copulates his words together and tears his heart asunder.

The next great dramatist is Sophocles. Æschylus had found Greek tragedy in a cart, under the charge of Thespis, a man of great consideration in his day, but of whom nothing remains to us, and he made it into the regular drama. Sophocles completed the work; he was of a more cultivated and chastened mind than Æschylus. He translated it into a choral peal of melody. Æschylus only excels in his grand bursts of feeling. The Antigone of Sophocles is the finest thing of the kind ever sketched by man.

Euripides, the next great dramatist, who has sometimes been likened to Racine, and sometimes to Corneille (although I cannot see much resemblance to Corneille at least), carried his compositions occasionally to the very verge of disease, and displays a distinct commencement of the age of speculation and scepticism. He **writes often for** *the effect's sake*, not as Homer or Æschylus, rapt away in the train of action; but how touching is effect so produced. He was accused of impiety. In a sceptical kind of man these two things go together very often—impiety and *desire of effect*. There is a decline in all kinds of literature when it ceases to be poetical and becomes speculative. Socrates was the emblem of the decline of the Greeks. His was the mind of the Greeks in its transition state; he was the friend of Euripides. It seems strange to call him so. I willingly admit that he was a man of deep feeling and morality; but I can well understand the idea which Aristophanes had of him, that he was a man going to destroy all Greece with his innovations. To understand this, we have only to go back to what I said in my last lecture on the peculiar character of the Greek system of religion—the crown of all their beliefs. The Greek system, you will remember, was of a great significance and value for the Greeks. Even the most absurd-looking part of the whole, the

D

Oracle, this too, was shown to have been not a quackery, but the result of a sincere belief on the part of the priests themselves. No matter what you call the process, if the man believed in what he was about, and listened to his faith in a higher power, surely by looking into himself, apart from earthly feeling, he would be in that frame of mind by far the best adapted for judging correctly and wisely of the future. They saw the most pious, intelligent, and reverend among them join themselves to this system, and thus was formed a sort of rude pagan church to the people. There were also the Greek games, celebrated in honour of the gods, and under the Divine sanction. We shall find that the Greek religion, in short, did essential service to the Greeks. The mind of the whole nation by its means obtained a strength and coherence. If I may not be permitted to say that through it all the nation became united to the Divine Power, I may, at any rate, assert that the highest considerations and motives thus became familiar to each person, and were put at the very top of his mind; but about Socrates' time this devotional feeling had in a great measure given way. He himself was not more sceptical than the rest; he shows a lingering kind of awe and attachment for the old religion of his country, and often we cannot make out whether he believed in it or not. He must have had but a painful intellectual life—a painful kind of life altogether, one would think. He was the son of a statuary, and was originally brought up in that art;

but he soon forsook it, and appeared to give up all doings with the world excepting such as would lead to its spiritual improvement. From that time he devoted himself to the teaching of morality and virtue, and he spent his life in that kind of mission. I cannot say that there was any evil in this; but it does seem to me to have been of a character entirely unprofitable. I have a great desire to admire Socrates, but I confess that his writings seem to be made up of a number of very wire-drawn notions about virtue. There is no conclusion in him; there is no word of life in Socrates! He was, however, personally a coherent and firm man. After him the nation became more and more sophistical. The Greek genius lost its originality; it lost its poetry, and gave way to the spirit of speculation. Alexander the Great subdued them, and though they fought well under him, and though manufactures and so forth flourished for a long time afterwards, not another man of genius of any very remarkable quality appeared in Greece.

LECTURE III.

May 7th.

FIRST PERIOD—*continued*.

THE ROMANS: THEIR CHARACTER, THEIR FORTUNE, WHAT THEY DID—FROM VIRGIL TO TACITUS—END OF PAGANISM.

We have now been occupied some two days in endeavouring to obtain a view of the practical, spiritual way of life among the Greeks. I shall now endeavour to draw this matter to a conclusion, the survey of the most ancient period of this our Western Europe.

We pass now to the Romans. We may say of this nation that, as the Greeks may be called the *children* of antiquity, from their *naïveté* and gracefulness, while their whole history is an aurora, the dawn of a higher culture and civilisation; so the Romans were the *men* of antiquity, and their history a glorious, warm, laborious day, less beautiful and graceful, no doubt, than the Greeks, but most essentially useful.

We have small time or space to enter largely into the discussion of Roman ways of thinking; but it is a fortunate coincidence that the Romans, in their special aspect, do not require much discussion. The Roman life and the Roman opinions are quite a sequel to those of the Greeks—a second edition, we may say, of the Pagan system of belief and action. As authors or promulgators of books, they will require comparatively little of our attention.

The first appearance of the Romans, their entering on the succession of the Greeks, is very picturesque. The Tarentines did certainly send—these, too, were Greeks, from of old inhabitants of Magna Græcia, of which I spoke in my first lecture—the Tarentines sent certainly embassies to Pyrrhus, the king of Epirus, in the year 280 B.C. He was an ambitious, martial prince, bent on conquering everybody, and therefore well suited for their wishes; they entreated him to come over and assist them against a people called Romans—some barbarians of that name. Pyrrhus embarked, landed, and gave battle to the Romans. According to Plutarch, when he saw them forming themselves in order of battle, he said, 'Why, these barbarians do not fight like barbarians!' and he accordingly afterwards found out to his cost that they did not fight like barbarians at all. A few years later he was worsted by the Romans, and again after that his forces were completely destroyed in another engagement. He himself said that, 'with him for their general and Romans for soldiers, he would conquer the world.'

One hundred years after this Greece itself was

completely subdued by the Romans; in the year before Christ 280 the war with Pyrrhus occurred. The Greek life was shattered to pieces against the harder, stronger life of the Romans. Corinth was taken and destroyed. Greece had degenerated; 100 years before Alexander, when Socrates died, we saw symptoms of not at all a healthy state of Greek existence; and now, as Corinth was taken and burned, and even Egypt with her Ptolemies, and Antioch with her Seleucidæ, fell successively into the power of the Romans, it was just as a beautiful crystal jar becomes dashed to pieces upon the hard rocks, so inexpressible was the force of the strong Roman energy. According to their own account they had already been established 280 years before that event, or 750 B.C.; but nothing is certainly known of them before that time. It is now pretty well understood that their ancient historians were all Greeks, who adopted the annals of those who conquered them. Not long ago that which had been already suspected by antiquarians and learned men was made good to demonstration by a German scholar, of whom you have no doubt all heard, Niebuhr, that all that story in Livy of Romulus and Remus, the two infants who were thrown into the Tiber and stranded on its banks, it being then the time of flood, and their being suckled by a she-wolf, and also that story of the kings Tarquin, are nothing after all but a *myth*, or traditional tale, with a few faint vestiges of meaning in it, but of no significance for the historian; at least, it refuses to yield it up to him. As to Niebuhr himself, he has accumulated a vast quantity of quotations and other materials, and, in short, his book is altogether a laborious thing; but he affords, after all, very little light on that early period. One does not find that he makes any conclusion out except destruction; and, after a laborious perusal of his work, we are forced to come to the conclusion that Niebuhr knew no more of the history of that period than I do.

No doubt *some human individual* built a house for himself in the neighbourhood of what must have then been a desert, overgrown with trees and shrubs—perhaps near to the old fountain, called afterwards the Fountain of Juturna, and probably even then in existence—one of the old fountains of the earth; but who he was, or how the work went on, we do not know, except that it became the most famous town in the world except Jerusalem, and destined to make the largest records of any town. Niebuhr has shown that the Romans evince the characters of two distinct species of people. First, there are the Pelasgi, a people inhabiting the lower part of Italy from of old; the same race as we have seen in Greece, where they had already become Hellenes. Secondly, there were the Etruscans or Tuscans, an entirely different race. Johannes von Müller supposes them to be northern Teutonic or Gothic. They are known by various remains of art, the terra cotta, baked earth. Winkelmann describes these remains to be of an Egyptian character from their gloomy heaviness, austerity, and sullenness. To the last moment the Etruscans continued to be the Haruspices of the Romans. They themselves were men of a gloomy character, very different from the liveliness and gracefulness of the Greeks. In the Romans we have the traces of these two races joined together; the one formed the noblesse, the other the commonalty. The main feature, independently of their works of art, which we observe in the old Etruscans is that they were an agricultural people, endowed with a sort of sullen energy, which is shown by the way in which they drained out lakes and marshes encumbering the soil, and these drains, I am told, are to be traced still; and in the Roman agricultural writers, such as Cato, Varro, and Columella, we meet with many old precepts which seem quite traditional.

We gather from these sources evidence of an intensely industrious thrift, a kind of vigorous thrift which was in that people. Thus, with respect to the ploughing of the earth, they express it to be a kind of blasphemy against Nature to leave a clod unbroken, and I believe that it is considered still to be good husbandry to pulverise the soil as much as possible. Now this feeling was the fundamental characteristic of the Roman people before they were distinguished as conquerors.

Thrift is a quality held in no esteem, and is generally regarded as mean; it is certainly mean enough, and objectionable from its interfering with all manner of intercourse between man and man.

But I say that thrift, well understood, includes in itself the best virtues that a man can have in this world; it teaches him self-denial, to postpone the present to the future, to calculate his means and to regulate his actions accordingly. Thus understood, it includes all that man can do in his vocation. Even in its worst state it indicates a great people, I think. The Dutch, for example (there is no stronger people), the people of New England, the Scotch — all great nations! In short, it is the foundation of all manner of virtue in a nation. Connected with this principle, there was in the Roman character a great seriousness and devoutness, and it was natural that there should be. The Greek religion was light and sportful compared to the Roman. The Roman deities were innumerable; Varro enumerates 30,000 divinities. Their notion of fate, which we observed was the central element of Paganism, was much more productive of consequences than the Greek notion, and it depended entirely on the original character which had been given to this people. Their notion was that Rome was always meant to be the capital of the whole world; that right was on the side of every man who was with Rome, and that therefore it was their duty to do everything for Rome. This belief tended very principally to produce its own fulfilment; nay, it was itself founded on fact. 'Did not Rome do so and so?' they would reason. That stubborn grinding down of the globe which their ancestors practised—ploughing the ground fifteen times to make it produce a better crop than if it were ploughed fourteen times was afterwards carried on by the Romans in all the concerns of their ordinary life, and by it they raised themselves above all other people.

Method was their great principle, just as harmony was that of the Greeks. The method of the Romans was a sort of harmony, but not that beautiful, graceful thing which was the Greek harmony. Theirs was the harmony of plans—an architectural harmony, which was displayed in the arranging of practical antecedents and consequences. Their whole genius was practical. Speculation with them was nothing in the comparison. Their vocation was not to teach the sciences—what sciences they knew they had received from the Greeks—but to teach practical wisdom; to subdue people into polity. Pliny declares that he cannot describe Rome. 'So great is it that it appears to make heaven more illustrious, and to bring the whole world into civilisation and obedience under its authority.' This is what it did. It had gone on for 300 years, fighting obscurely with its neighbours, and getting one state after another into its power, when the defeat of Pyrrhus gave it all Italy, and rendered that country entirely Rome. Some have thought that the Romans had done nothing else but fight to establish their dominion where they had not the least claim of right, and that they were a mere nest of robbers; but this is evidently a misapprehension. Historians have generally managed to write down such facts as are apt to strike the memory of the vulgar, while they omit the circumstances which display the real character of the Romans. The Romans were at first an agricultural people. They built, it appears, their barns within their walls for protection; but they got incidentally into quarrels with other neighbouring states, and it is not strange that they should have taken the opportunity to compel them by force to adopt their civilisation, such as it was, in preference to the mere foolish and savage method of their own. I do not mean to say that the Roman was a mild kind of discipline; far from that. It was established only by hard contests and fighting; but it was of all the most beneficial. In spite of all that has been said and ought to be said about liberty, it is true liberty to obey the best personal guidance, either out of our own head or out of that of some other. No one would wish to see some fool wandering about at his own will, and without any restraint or direction; we must admit it to be far better for him if some wise man were to take charge of him, even though by force, although that seems but a coarse kind of operation. But fighting was not at all the fundamental principle in their conquests; it was their superior civilisation which attracted the surrounding nations to their centre. If their course had been entirely unwise, all the world would have risen in arms against the domineering tyrants for ever claiming to be their rulers where they had no right at all, and their power could not have subsisted there as it did.

After they had conquered Pyrrhus, and before their conflict, which took place a century after that, with Greece, the event occurred which was the crowning phenomenon of their history. They found their way into the neighbouring island of Sicily, and there they met with the Carthaginians, another ancient state, of great power and prosperity, and, as far as probabilities went, more likely to subject the whole world than Rome herself was. But it was not so ordered. A collision ensued between them, which lasted 120 years, and constituted the three Punic Wars. It **was the** hardest struggle Rome ever had—the hardest that ever was. The Carthaginians were as obstinate a people as the Romans themselves. They were of the race called Punic, Phœnic, or Phœnician, an Oriental people of the family now called Semitic because descended from Sem; the same kind of people as the **Jews**, and as distinguished as Jews for being a stiff-necked people. I most sincerely rejoice that they did not subdue the Romans, but that the Romans got the better of them. We have indications which show that, compared to the Romans, they were a mean people, who thought of nothing but commerce, would do anything for money, and were exceedingly cruel in their measures of **aggrandisement**, and in all their measures. Their **rites were of a** kind perfectly horrid; their religion **was of that** sort so often denounced in the Bible, with which the Jews were to have nothing to do. In the siege of Carthage the Romans relate that they offered their children to Bel, who is the same as Moloch, 'making them to pass through the fire unto Moloch,' in the language of Scripture, for they had a statue of the god in metal, which was heated red-hot, and they flung these hapless wretches into his outspread arms. Their injustice was proverbial; the expression 'Punic faith' was well justified by the facts. This people, however, determined to exert their whole strength against the Romans.

Hannibal, whom Napoleon conceived to be the greatest captain, the greatest soldier of antiquity, was certainly a man of wonderful talent and tenacity, maintaining himself for sixteen years in Italy in spite of all the Roman power. He was scandalously treated on his return by his own countrymen. He was a most unfortunate man; banished from Carthage, and at last, to prevent his falling into the hands of his enemies, the Romans, he had no resource but poisoning himself. Carthage, however, was taken, and was burned for six days. It reminds us of the destruction of Jerusalem; for, as I have observed, the Jews have always distinguished themselves with the same tenacity and obstinacy, clinging to the same belief, probable or improbable, or even impossible. How the Romans got on after that we can see by the Commentaries which Julius Cæsar has left us of his own proceedings, how he spent ten years of campaigns in Gaul cautiously planning all his measures before he attempted to carry them into effect. It is, indeed, a most interesting book, and evinces the indomitable force of Roman energy. The triumph of civil, methodic man over wild and barbarous man; of calm, patient discipline over that valour which is without direction, which is ready to die if necessary, but knows nothing further than that.

Notwithstanding what writers have said, it is clear that no one understands what the Roman Constitution actually was. Niebuhr has attempted it, but he throws no light at all upon the subject, and I think that in the absence of information to draw any inferences on one side or the other is extremely unwise. It appears to have been a very tumultuous kind of polity, a continual struggle between the Patricians and Plebeians, the latter of whom were bent on having the lands of the State equally divided between them and the upper orders. We read of constant secessions to the Aventine, and there was rough work very frequently. Therefore, I cannot join in the lamentations made by some over the downfall of the Republic when Cæsar took hold of it. It had been but a constant struggling scramble for prey, and it was well to end it, and to see the wisest, cleanest, and most judicious man of them place himself at the top of it. The Romans under the empire attained to their complete grandeur, their dominion reached from the river Euphrates away to Cadiz, from the border of the Arabian desert to Severus' Wall up in the north of England. And what an empire it was! teaching mankind that they should be tilling the ground, as they ought to do, instead of fighting one another! For that is the real thing which every man is called on to do, to till the ground, and not slay his poor brother man.

Coming now to their literature we find it to be a copy of that of the Greeks, but there is a kind of Roman worth in many of their books. Their language, too, has a character belonging to Rome. Etymologists have traced many words in it to the Pelasgic, and some have been followed out so far as the Sanskrit, proving thus the existence in the Romans of the two kinds of blood which I have indicated. Its peculiarly distinguishing character, however, is its imperative sound and structure, finely adapted to command.

So in their books, as, for instance, the poems of Virgil and Horace, we see the Roman character of a still strength. But their greatest work was written on the face of the planet in which we live. Their Cyclopean highways, extending from country to country, their aqueducts, their Coliseums, their whole polity! And how spontaneous all these things were! how little any Roman knew what Rome was!

There is a tendency in all historians to place a plan in the head of every one of their great characters, by which he regulated his actions, forgetting that it is not possible for any man to have foreseen events, and to have embraced at once the vast complication of the circumstances that were to happen.

It is more reasonable to attribute national progress to a great, deep instinct in every individual actor. Who of **us**, for example, knows England, though **he may** contribute to her prosperity? Every one **here follows his** own object; one goes to India, another aspires to the army, and each after his **own** ends; but all thus co-operate together after all, one Englishman with another, in adding to the strength and wealth of the whole nation. The wisest government has only to direct this spirit into a proper channel, but to believe that it can lay down a plan for the creation of national enterprise is an **entire folly.** These incidents form the deep foundation of a national character; when they fail the nation fails too, just as when the roots of a tree fail and the sap can mount the trunk and diffuse **itself among the** leaves no longer, the tree stops too.

During a healthy, sound, progressive period of national existence **there** is in general no literature at all.

In a time of active exertion the nation will not speak out its mind. It is not till a nation is ready to decline that its literature makes itself remarkable, and this is observable in all nations, for there are many ways in which a man or a nation expresses itself besides books. The point is not to be able to write a book, the **point is** *to have the true mind* for **it.** Everything in that case which the nation does will be equally significant of its mind. If any great man **among** the Romans, Julius Cæsar or Cato for example, had **never** done anything but till the ground they would have acquired equal excellence in that way. They would have ploughed as they conquered. Everything a great man does carries the traces of a great man. Perhaps even there is the most energetic **virtue** when there is no talk about virtue at all. I wish my friends here to consider and keep this in view, that progress and civilisation may go on unknown to the people themselves, that there may be **a primeval feeling** of energy and virtue in the founders of a state whether they can fathom it or not. This feeling gets **nearer** every generation to be uttered, for though the son learns only such things as his father has invented, yet he will discover other things, and teach as well his own as his father's inventions in his turn to his children, and so it will go on working itself out till it gets into conversation and speech. We shall observe precisely this when we come to the reign of **Queen** Elizabeth. All great things in short, whether **national** or individual, **are** unconscious things! I cannot get room to insist on this here, but we shall see them as we go on, **like** seeds thrown out upon a wide fertile field; no man sees what they are, but they grow up before us and become great.

What did that man when **he** built his house know of Rome **or** of Julius Cæsar that were to come? They were the product of time! Fust, of Mentz, **who** invented printing, that subject of so much admiration in our times, never thought of the results that were to follow; he found it a cheaper

E

way of publishing his Bibles, and he used it for no other purpose than to undersell the other booksellers. In short, from the Christian religion down to the poorest genuine song there has been no consciousness in the minds of the first authors of anything of excellence. Shakespeare, too, never seemed to imagine that he had any talent at all, his only object seems to have been to gather a little money, for he was very necessitous; and when we do find consciousness the thing done is sure to be not a great thing at all; it is a very suspicious circumstance when anything makes a great noise about itself; it is like a drum, producing a great deal of sound, but very like to be empty.

I shall here take a short survey of Roman books. The poem of Virgil, the Æneid, has long enjoyed, and will continue to enjoy, a great reputation. It ranks as an Epic poem, and one, too, of the same sort of name as the Iliad of Homer. But I think it entirely a different poem, and very inferior to Homer. There is that fatal consciousness, that knowledge that he is writing an epic, the plot, the style, all is vitiated by that one fault! The characters, too, are none of them to be compared to the healthy, whole-hearted, robust men of Homer, the 'much-enduring' Ulysses, or Achilles, or Agamemnon. Æneas, the hero of the poem, is a lachrymose sort of man altogether. He is introduced in the middle of a storm, but instead of handling the tackle and doing what he can for the ship he sits still, groaning over his misfortunes!

'Was ever mortal,' he asks, 'so unfortunate as I am? chased from port to port by the persecuting Deities who give me no respite!' and so on. And then he tells them how that he is the 'pious Æneas,' in short, he is just that sort of lachrymose man there is hardly anything of a man in the inside of him. But Virgil succeeded much better in his other poems. This Æneid is not a fair sample of what he could do; his descriptions of natural scenery are very beautiful, and he was a great poet when he did not observe himself, and when he let himself alone.

His poetry is soft and sweet. In his women, too, he succeeded wonderfully; his Dido was unmatched by anything that had gone before. He was a mild and gentle man, born poor, and the son of a peasant. He got his education from his father, and he cultivated his paternal inheritance, but being dispossessed by some soldiers, as he himself tells us, of his estate, he had to go to Rome about it; this was the beginning of his fortune. He became known to Mecænas, and afterwards to Augustus. He was a man of mild deportment, insomuch that the people of Naples, with whom he lived, used to call him 'the Maid.' He was an amiable man, and always in bad health, much subject to dyspepsia, and to all kinds of maladies that afflict men of genius. The effect of his poetry is like that of some laborious mosaic of many years in putting together. There is also the Roman method, the Roman amplitude and regularity, just as these qualities were exhibited in the empire, but entirely without that abandonment of self which Homer had. His sentiments and descriptive sketches are often borrowed out of Homer or Theocritus, but the style and the poetry of the whole overspreading the work with a beautiful enamel enable us to judge of what he might have been had he less studied to produce effect. We must, however, conclude that he was, properly speaking, not an Epic poet.

Of Horace I can afford to say almost nothing. He, too, was a sort of friend of Cæsar. His was a similar history to that of Virgil, and, like him, he was not betrayed into perverseness by the possession of great wealth. There was in him the same polish, 'a curious felicity,' as one person expresses it. I cannot admire always his moral philosophy. He is sometimes not at all edifying in his sentiments. He belonged to the Epicurean school of philosophy, an unbelieving man, with no thought for anything but how to make himself comfortable, and to enjoy himself in this world; until a dark melancholy comes over him, at which time his opinions appear in their most respectable shape, and then he sees the all-devouring death expecting him, he knows well with what issues, and at last takes refuge from the contemplation in Epicurean enjoyment. In his writings he displays a worldly kind of sagacity, but it is a great sagacity!

It is remarkable how soon afterwards Roman literature had quite degenerated. Ovid, the next celebrated poet, has an ever-present consciousness of himself, and is very inferior to Horace or Virgil. From this time we get more and more into self-consciousness and into scepticism, and not long afterwards without being able to find any bottom at all to it. I refer to Seneca and Lucan, his nephew, and the whole family of Senecas. Seneca was originally from Cordova in Spain; he got into politics, and he was Nero's master or tutor.

He has left some works on philosophy, and there are some tragedies (twelve, I think) which go by his name. Some of these are said to have been written by his nephew, Lucan; at all events, they were written by one of Seneca's school, and fully imbued with his philosophy. Now, if we want an example of a diseased self-consciousness, an exaggerated imagination, a mind blown up with all sorts of strange conceits, the spasmodic state of intellect, in short, of a man morally unable to speak the truth on any subject, we have it in Seneca. He was led away by this strange humour into all sorts of cant and insincerity. He exaggerated the virtues, for instance, to an extreme quite ridiculous, asserting that there is no such thing as vice at all, that man is all powerful and like to a god in this world, having it in his power to triumph over evils and calamities of all kinds by his mere will; and all this while Seneca himself was a mere pettifogging courtier, careful of nothing but amassing money, and flattering Nero in all his ways. Indeed, it is impossible to read such writings as he has left us without suspecting something. We cannot help saying, 'All is not right here.' I willingly admit that he had a strong desire to be sincere, and that he endeavoured to convince himself that he was right; but even this, when in connexion with the rest, constitutes of itself a fault of a dangerous kind. We may trace it all to that same spirit of self-conceit, pride, and vanity, which is the ruin of all things in this world, and always will be. The vices of this kind of literature connect themselves in a natural sequence with the decline of Roman virtue altogether, when that people had once come to disbelief in their own gods, and to put all their confidence in their money, believing that with their money they could always buy their money's worth.

This order of things was closely succeeded by moral abominations of the most dreadful kind, such as were not known before nor ever since, the most fearful abominations under the sun. But it is curious to observe that such is the power of genius to make itself heard and felt in all times that the most significant and the greatest of Roman writers occurs posterior to these times of Seneca—I mean Tacitus. In those extraordinary circumstances of his times he displays more of the Roman spirit, perhaps, than any one before him. His mind was not hid under all that black mass of blasphemy, covetousness, and villainy. He shows it in his estimate of the Germans even, for it was something new for any Roman to speak favourably of barbarians, or to hold any other opinion of their fellowmen than that every man was born to be a slave to Rome. In the Germans he sees a kind of worth, and seems to contemplate with a kind of shuddering anticipation the time when these Germans were to come and sweep away his corrupted country. 'The Germans,' he says, 'wage a continual war with one another; may the gods grant that it may always be so.' In the middle of all those facts in the literature of his country, which correspond so well with what we know of the history of Rome itself, in the middle of all that quackery and puffery coming into play, when critics wrote books to teach you how to hold out your arm and your leg, in the middle of all this absurd and wicked period, Tacitus was born, and was enabled to be a Roman after all! He stood like a Colossus at the edge of a dark night, and he sees events of all kinds hurrying past him and plunging he knows not where, but evidently to no good, for falsehood and cowardice never yet ended anywhere but in destruction. He sees all this and narrates it with grave calmness, giving us quietly his notions of Tiberius and others, and, as he goes on, he does not seem startled, but full of deep views, unable to account for it but convinced that it will end well somehow or other, for he has no belief but the old Roman belief, full of their old feelings of goodness and honesty. He is greatly distinguished from all of that time, greatly distinguished from Livy, who has collected together all the soft and beautiful myths of the time and woven them into a highly interesting history; but, as a historian, he was a far inferior man to Tacitus.

I shall now quit the subject of Pagan literature, for after Tacitus all things went on sinking down more and more into all kinds of disease and ruin. After the survey which we have made, we come to the conclusion that there is a strange coherence between the healthy belief and outward destiny of a nation. Thus the Greeks went on with their wars and everything else most prosperously till they became conscious of their condition—till the man became solicitous after other times. Socrates, we saw, is a kind of starting-point, from which we trace their fall into confusion and wreck of all sorts. So it was with the Romans. Cato the Elder used to tell them: 'The instant you get the Greek literature among you there will be an end of the old Roman spirit.' He was not listened to; the rage for Greek speculation increased; he himself found it impossible to keep back, although he was very angry about it, and in his old age he learnt the Greek language and had it taught to his sons. It was too late; nobody could believe any longer, and every one had set his mind upon being a man and thinking for himself. In the middle of all that the event occurred, which I shall repeat in the language of Tacitus, who, after mentioning that in the reign of Nero Rome was set on fire, and, as was said, by order of that prince, who did it most probably because he wished to build some new streets and disliked to take the trouble of clearing away the old houses in any other manner, and that he sat playing his harp and watching the fire, whereupon a great rumour became raised abroad, goes on to say, as I have almost literally rendered it from the Ann. xv. chap. 44 :—

'So for the abolishing of that rumour he caused to be indicted and afterwards punished with exquisite pains a people hated for their wickedness (*per flagitia invisos*), whom the vulgar called Christians. The author of that sect was one Christ (*Christus quidam*), who, in the reign of Tiberius, was put to death by the procurator of Syria, Pontius Pilate, for his hateful superstition (*propter exitiale superstitione*), whereby being for a time suppressed, it broke out again not only in Judæa, where it first arose, but spread itself also unto other countries, and finally unto Rome itself, where all things wicked and horrible come at last to gather themselves together.'

Tacitus lived eighty-eight years after the events which he here describes. It was given to him to see no deeper into the matter than appears from the above account of it. But he and the great empire were soon to pass away for ever!—and it was in this despised sect—this *Christus quidam*—it was in this new character that all the future world lay hid!

This will furnish us with the subject of our next lecture.

LECTURE IV.

May 11*th*.

SECOND PERIOD.

MIDDLE AGES—CHRISTIANITY; FAITH—INVENTIONS—PIOUS FOUNDATIONS—POPE HILDEBRAND—CRUSADES—TROUBADOURS—NIEBELUNGEN LIED.

We have now to direct our attention to a ruder state of man, and we shall observe with what shrewdness man will in this state lay hold of the information and civilisation afforded him. For we have traced our subject through the Old World, and now we come to the New; we investigated, first among the Greeks and next among the Romans, the system of Polytheism and Paganism. We have now an equal period of history to survey, that of the modern era, for about 1800 years from the birth of Christ; having already passed through as much before that epoch as we are now from it. We shall, therefore, commence with what we can call the Transition Period, or period of the formation of this present life of man, that in which all our beliefs and our general way of existence shape themselves. The Middle Ages used to be called ages of darkness, rudeness, and barbarity, 'the Millennium of Darkness,' as one writer calls them; but it is universally apparent now that these ages are not to be so called. The only writers in the early part of those times—times of convulsions, cruel periods—were Romans. The barbarians who rushed out into the scene of conquest were not given to writing, and accordingly these writers indulge in much abuse of their invaders and wild lamentation, recounting the fall of their empire with a dense shriek of horror and indignation. With them, therefore, the name of barbarian is a synonym for whatever is bad and base; to this day the name of 'Goth' is so applied, even with us, the descendants of those conquerors. It was a great and fertile period, however—that invasion of the barbarians and their settlement in the Roman Empire. There is a sentence which I find in Goethe, full of meaning in this regard. It must be noted, he says, 'that belief and unbelief are two opposite principles in human nature. The theme of all human history, so far as we are able to perceive it, is the contest between these two principles.' 'All periods,' he goes on to say, 'in which belief predominates, in which it is the main element, the inspiring principle of action, are distinguished by great, soul-stirring, fertile events, and worthy of perpetual remembrance. And, on the other hand, when unbelief gets the upper hand, that age is unfertile, unproductive, and intrinsically mean; in which there is no pabulum for the spirit of man, and no one can get nourishment for himself!' This passage is one of the most pregnant utterances ever delivered, and we shall do well to keep it in mind in these disquisitions on this period; for in the Middle Ages we see the great phenomenon of belief gaining the victory over unbelief. And this same remark is altogether true of all things whatever in this world, and it throws much light on the history of the whole world, and that in two ways, for belief serves both as a fact itself and the cause of other facts. It appears only in a healthy mind, and it is at once an indication of it and the cause of it. For though doubt may be necessary to a certain extent in order to prepare subject-matter for reflection, it can be only after all a morbid condition of the intellect, and an intermediate one; but that speculation should *end* in doubt is wholly unreasonable. It is, as I have said, a *morbid* state; it is a state of mental paralysis—a highly painful state of mind, one which the healthy man won't entertain at all, but, if he can do nothing better with it, dismisses it altogether. There is no use in it that one can understand except to give the mind something to work on. Belief, then, is the indication and the cause of health, and when we see it in a whole world we may be sure that the world is able to say and to do something. It is the heart rather than the intellect that Goethe has in mind in the passage quoted. It is the heart after all that most influences. Our knowledge of physics, our whole circle of scientific acquirements, depends on what figure each man will give it and shape to himself in his own heart!

Thus in the Middle Ages, being in contact with fact and reality, in communion with truth and nature, not merely with hearsays and vain formulas, but feeling the presence of truth in the heart, that is the great fact of the time—belief! And this is independent of their dogmas. In the genuine Pagan times, too, among much that is absurd and reprehensible, we found a great good accomplished by its means; there was there also a belief, which was accompanied by an adjustment of themselves towards these opinions of theirs. They had discovered and recognised in themselves, whether they expressed it in words or not, the existence of a Supreme Arrangement; they had not discovered it without perceiving the numerous inconsistencies and contradictions of their religious system; these had doubtless struck them at first, but they had adjusted themselves to that; but their way of religion and life had this kind of belief in it—*belief in one's self!* They did not fail to observe what a thing man is—what a high, royal nature is given to him! This appears in particular in later times, when the old religion had altogether passed away, and its intellectual results only remained, in their philosophers, for instance, and strikingly above all others in the Stoics, a set extremely prevalent in Rome; in later times all that the Romans had to adhere to in the way of belief.

One sees in their opinions a great truth, but

extremely exaggerated: that bold assertion, for example, in the face of all reason and fact, that pain and pleasure are the same thing; that man is indifferent to both; that he is a king in this world; that nothing can conquer him! Still more strikingly is it displayed in a peculiar sort of Stoicism, the Cynic set of philosophers. There have been few more striking characters than that of Diogenes the Cynic, adopting the Stoic principle and carrying it out to its extreme development, and professing to set himself above all accidental circumstances, such as poverty or disgrace, and taking them rather as a sort of schooling, as a lesson he was to learn and in the best manner he could. D'Alembert pronounces him to have been one of the greatest men of antiquity, although there were in him several things counter to D'Alembert's way of thinking; decency, for example, was of no significance for him. It is strange to see that remarkable interview—the one the conqueror of all the world, in his pride and glory and splendour; the other a poor needy man, with nothing beside his skin save the soul that was in him! Alexander asked him in their interview (for Diogenes had a sharp, sour tongue in his head) if he could give him anything? 'You can stand out of the sun and give me light.' That was all Alexander could give Diogenes! This was certainly a great thing, and altogether worthy to be recognised; it was much for man. But if we look into the Christian religion, that dignification of man's life and nature, we shall find, indeed, this also in it—to believe in one's self, that thing given to him by the Creator. But then how unspeakably more human is *this* belief, not held in proud scorn and contempt of other men, in cynical disdain or indignation at their paltrinesses, but received by exterminating pride altogether from the mind, and held in degradation and deep human sufferings. There is darkness and affliction in all things around it in its origin. We saw what it appeared to Tacitus, the greatest man of his time, some seventy years after its origin. Its outward history was on a par with its interior meaning; its province was not to encourage pride, but to cut that down altogether. There is a remarkable passage of Goethe, where he calls it 'the worship of Sorrow,' its doctrine 'the sanctuary of Sorrow.' It was, he continues (regarding it simply on its secular side, not in view of any particular religious sect, but just as the Divinest thing that could be looked at), the showing to man for the first time that suffering and degradation, the most hateful to the sensual regard, possessed a beauty which surpassed all other beauty. It is not our part to touch on sacred things, but we should altogether fail to discover the meaning of this Historical Period if we did not lay deeply to heart the meaning of Christianity. In another point of view we may regard it as the revelation of eternity existing in the middle of time to man. He stands here between the conflux of two elements, the Past and the Future; the thing that we are at this moment speaking or doing comes to us from the beginning of days. The word I am this moment speaking came to me from Cadmus of Thebes, or some other ancient member of the great family of Adam, and it will go on to an endless future!

Every man may with truth say that he waited for a whole eternity to be born, and that he has now a whole eternity waiting to see what he will do now that he is born. It is this which gives to this little period of life, so contemptible when weighed against eternity, a significance it never had without it. It is thus an infinite arena, where infinite interests are played out; not an action of man but will have its truth realised and will go on for ever. His most insignificant action, for some are more so than others, carries its print of this endless duration.

This truth, whatever may be the opinions we hold on Christian doctrines, or whether we hold upon them a sacred silence or not, we must recognise in Christianity and its belief, independently of all theories, for it was not revealed till then, and it is not possible to imagine results of a more significant nature than those it produced. One can fancy with what mute astonishment the invading barbarians must have paused when their wild barbarous minds were first saluted with the tidings of that great Eternity lying round the world, this earth now become an intelligible thing to them; how this wild German people, heated with conquest and tumult, paused and took it all in, this doctrine, without argument. I believe that argument was not at all used; it was done by the conviction of the men themselves, who spoke into convincible minds; and herein is the great distinction of ancient from modern Europe, nay, of modern Europe from all the world besides.

It has been truly said by Goethe that this is a progress that we are all capable of making and destined to make, and from which, when made, we can never retrograde. There may be all manner of arguments and delusions, and true and false speculations about it; but we can well understand the Divine doctrine of Eternity, manifesting itself in time, and time drawing all its meaning from eternity. It only requires a pure heart, and then if all else were destroyed, if there were even no Bible, and a mere tradition remaining of its having once been, from the progress once made, we should never go back. If to this sublime proceeding we add the character of the northern people—the German people, best suited of all others to receive the faith and maintain it and develop it, being endowed with the largest nature, the deepest affections; if, I say, we add these together, we shall have the two leading phenomena of the Middle Ages, the possibility of great nations constructing themselves, and of all good things coming out of them. It is curious accordingly to see with what facility the matter proceeds; in two centuries after the people of the North had begun to break in on the South, from Alaric downwards, how quietly do all things settle down into arrangement, in one just way, everything with a new character of its own, and all displaying that shrewdness which, to refer to the text with which we set out, marks the intellectual efforts of societies in their rude state.

There was that thing which we call loyalty. That attachment of **man** to man, indeed, is as old as the existence of man himself. The kings and chiefs of early times had their dependents; Achilles, for example, had his Myrmidons. The feeling must exist among men if they are to maintain themselves in society. At the same time, it **had never** before nor anywhere existed in such a shape as it has since assumed among the modern **nations** of Europe, **the** descendants **of the** Romans and Germans, men of the deepest affections, and imbued with the sacred principle of Christianity; in them resulting in every thing great and noble, and in this feeling of *loyalty* among others. In these times loyalty is **much** kept out of sight and little appreciated, and many minds regard it as a sort of obsolete chimera, looking more to independence or **some** such thing now regarded as a great virtue; and **this is very** just, and most suitable to this time of movement and progress. It must be granted at once that to exact loyalty to things so bad as to be not worth being loyal to is quite an insupportable thing, and one that the world would spurn at once. This must be conceded; yet the better thinkers will see that loyalty is a principle perennial in human nature, the highest that unfolds itself there in a temporal, secular point of view; for there is no other kind of way by which human society can be safely constructed than that feeling of loyalty, whereby those who are worthy are reverenced by those who are capable of reverence. Thus, in the Middle Ages it was the noblest phenomenon, the finest phase in society anywhere. Loyalty was the foundation of the state.

Another great cardinal point, a hinge on which all other things were suspended, was the Church, the institution appointed to keep alive the sacred light of religion. No doubt the men of that age held many absurd doctrines, but we must remember that it is not scientific doctrines that constitute belief: it is the sincerity of *heart* which constitutes the whole merit of belief. Many of their doctrines, doubtless, were absurd and entirely incredible, but we shall blind ourselves to their significance if we do not see into them independently of theology. It is curious to trace the phenomena of the Christian Church in early days, how it grows on in neglect and indifference. Besides the remarkable passage out of Tacitus, which I read in my last lecture, we have another curious document probably a little later, the celebrated letter of Pliny to the Emperor Trajan respecting the Christians of Bithynia. It was written prior to the year 100 A.D., but there is no date to it. It is very striking to observe how, in the middle of that black night which then overspread the earth, of that great darkness, a small light begins to make itself seen! But Pliny could not see anything important in these people. He writes that 'certain people among them admit that they are Christians, some say that they were two or three years ago, but have since left them.' But some *did admit* that they were Christians. They were far, he goes on to say, from being given to lies and bad practices (*flagitia*, flagitious practices); they told him that they met together and exhorted one another on certain days (doubtless on the Christian Sabbath) before sunrise, precisely to avoid all that, and that after so exhorting themselves they met together at a friendly repast (doubtless this was the Communion). That they were quite free and unspotted, however, from the vices with which the world charged them, that world itself wholly immersed in those very vices! And he recommends that they should be let alone, and should not be persecuted, for he does not think that they will last much longer; they had agreed to give up meeting together, and to avoid all that would give offence. What is a very remarkable fact, he goes on to say that he thinks that they may go on with their opinions without danger to the State religion, for that he had been recently refitting the temples, and that they were now more crowded than ever they were, and, in short, that the old spirit was returning, and that everything would revive. This was the character of the Church down to the end of the first century. From that time churches began to spring up everywhere, synods were established, and bishops in every church; there is no doubt, too, that the seat of the main ecclesiastical power was at Rome, the Bishop of which city had a pre-eminence among the bishops. This became fully established under Gregory the Great.

At that time the name of the chief Bishop was not Pope but Primate. From Rome he sent his commands to all parts of the Christian world. He it was who sent the monk Augustine with a few other monks to this country, who converted our Saxon ancestors to Christianity. Like all other matters there were contradictions and inconsistencies without end, but it should be regarded in its ideal.

The greatest height to which it ever did attain in the world was in the time of Pope Hildebrand, about the year 1070, or soon after the conquest of England by William the Conqueror. That was its time of highest perfection. All Europe then was firm and unshaken in the faith. It abounded in churches, and monks, and convents, founded for meditation and silent study; that was the ideal of monachism. It was the age of teachers and preachers of all kinds, sent into all parts of the world to convert all the heathen into Christianity. It was the Church itself, for which human society was then constituted, for what were human things in comparison with the eternal world which lay beyond them. Hildebrand was, it appears, though not certainly, the son of a Tuscan peasant; he was a great and deep thinker, and at an early period he entered the monastic life, as it was natural he should, for there was no other congenial employment open to him. He became one of the monks in the famous monastery of Clugny. There he soon distinguished himself for his superior attainments, was successively promoted and employed by several Popes on missions of importance, and at last he became Pope himself. One can well see from his history what it was he meant. He has been regarded by some classes of Protestants as the wickedest of men, but I do hope that we have at this day outgrown all that. He perceived that the Church was the highest thing in the world, and he resolved that it should be at the top of the whole world, animating human things and giving them their main guidance. He first published the Decretal Order on the celibacy of the clergy, determined that they should have nothing to do with worldly affairs, **but** should work as soldiers enlisted in a sacred cause.

There was another pretension made by him, which, indeed, had been the subject of controversy before, but which Hildebrand put forward in quite a new light. That was, that popes, bishops, and priests had no right to be invested with their offices by the Emperor of Germany, or any temporal lord, but that being once nominated by the Church they were henceforth validly invested with their offices, and this was so because the world could have no legitimate control in things spiritual. The Emperor of Germany, at that time Henry IV., a young man **and** not of sufficient wisdom to know the age, resisted this pretension, and the Pope resisted him, and there ensued great quantities of confused struggling. At last, in the month of January 1077, at the castle of Canossa, now in ruins near Reggio in Modena, whither Hildebrand had retired after having excommunicated the Germans, and freed the Saxons then in arms against Henry's authority, Henry became reduced to the painful necessity of coming away to him, and offering to submit to any punishment the Pope should appoint. His reception was most humiliating; he was obliged to leave all his attendants at some distance, and come himself in the garb of a penitent with nothing on him but a woollen cloth, and there to stand for three days in the snow before he was suffered to come into the Pope's presence! One would think from all this that Hildebrand was a proud man, but he was not a proud man at all, and seems from many circumstances to have been, on the contrary, a man of very great humility; but here he treated himself as the representative of Christ, and far beyond all earthly authorities, and he reasoned that if Christ was higher than the Emperor the Emperor ought to subject himself to the Church's power as all Europe was obliged to do. In these circumstances, doubtless, there are many questionable things, but then there are many cheering things, for we see the son of a poor Tuscan peasant, solely by the superior spiritual force that was in him, humble a great Emperor at the head of the iron force of Europe! And to look at it in a tolerant point of view, it is really very grand, it is the spirit of Europe set above the body of Europe, mind triumphant **over** brute force!

Hildebrand endured great miseries after that; he was **for** three years besieged by Henry in the castle of **St.** Angelo until he died. Some have feared that **the** tendency of such things is to found **a** theocracy, and have imagined that if this had gone on till our days a most abject superstition would have become established. But this is **en**-tirely a vain theory. The clay that is about man is always sufficiently ready to assert its rights; the danger is always the other way, that the spiritual part of man will become overlaid with his bodily part.

This, then, was **the** Church. The Church and **the** loyalty **of** the time were the two hinges of **society**; **and** that society was in consequence distinguished from all societies which had preceded it, presenting an infinitely greater diversity of view, **a** better humanity, a largeness of capacity. This society has since undergone many changes, but I hope that spirit may go on for countless ages yet, the spirit which at that period was set going.

A strange phase of the healthy belief, the deep **belief** of the time, were the Crusades. I am far **from** vindicating the Crusades in a political point of view, but at the **same time** we should miss the grand apex of that life if we did not for a moment dwell upon these events. It was a strange thing to see how **Peter,** a **poor** monk, recently come home from Syria, but fully convinced of the propriety of the step, set out on his mission through Europe; how he talked about it to the Pope, regarding it as a proper and indispensably necessary duty to remove the abomination of Mahometanism from the sacred places, till in 1096 the Council of Clermont was held in Auvergne. One sees Peter riding along, dressed in his brown cloak, with the rope of the penitent tied round him, swaying all hearts and burning them up with zeal, and stirring up steel-clad Europe till it shook itself at his words. What a contrast to that greatest of orators, Demosthenes, spending nights and years in the construction of those balanced sentences which are still read with admiration, descending into the smallest details, speaking with pebbles in his mouth and the waves of the sea beside him; and all his way of life in this manner occupied during many years, and then to end in simply nothing at all, for he did nothing for his country with all his eloquence; and then see this poor monk start out here without any art at all, but with something far greater than art! For, as Demosthenes was once asked, what was the secret of a fine orator, and he replied, action! action! action! so, if I were asked it, I should say, belief! belief! belief! He must be first persuaded himself if he wish to persuade other people.

The Crusades altogether lasted upwards of 100 years; Jerusalem was taken in 1099. Some have admired them because they served to bring all

Europe into communication with itself, others because it produced the elevation of the middle classes; but I say that the great result which characterises them and gives them all their merit is, that in them Europe for one moment proved its belief, proved that it believed in the invisible world which surrounds the outward visible world; that this belief had for once entered into the circumstances of man! This fact that for once something sacred entered into the minds of nations, has been more productive of practical results than any other could be; it lives yet, transmitting itself by unseen channels as all good things do in this world.

In these ages it is not to be expected that there was any literature: it was a healthy age. We have remarked in the last lecture that the appearance of literature is a sign that the age producing it is not far from decline and decay. The great principles which animate its development are at work, deep and unconscious, long before they get to express themselves, and the people follow by instinct their commands. Literature could not exist in such a time when even the nobles and great men were unable to write. Their only mode of signing charters was by dipping the glove-mailed hand into the ink and imprinting it on the charter. A strong warrior would disdain to write, he had other functions than this; and though writing is one of the noblest utterances, for speech is so, there are other ways besides that of expressing one's self, and to lead a heroic life is, perhaps, a greater thing than to write a heroic poem! This was the case of the Middle Ages. I do not mean to say that the ideal of the age was perfect, far from that! No age that has yet been has not been one of contradictions, which make the heart sick and sore if the heart be earnest. But I assert that an ideal did exist; the heroic heart was not then desolate and alone, it was appreciated, and its great result was a perpetual struggling forward, that was the real age of gold! We know that in any other way there has never been such a thing as an age of gold. Nothing is to be won but by human exertions. But a literature did come at last. I allude to the Troubadours and Trouvères of the twelfth century. These will not detain us long. Theirs were the beautiful childlike utterances just waking to speak of chivalry, and heroic deeds, and love, in song and music: the people had begun to get able to speak then. This sort of poetry became not much improved afterwards, it was perfect from the first; indeed, it could not have received any improvement from succeeding times, for shortly afterwards we observe the rise of a kind of feeling adverse to this spirit of harmony, which we shall by-and-by see get out into Protestantism. In the meantime all was one beautiful harmony and religious unity. It is astonishing to see to what an extent music and singing had already gone in all countries. The Troubadours and Trouvères belonged to distinct races—the one Norman, with whom were joined our English forefathers; and the others, the Troubadours, were Provençal. This formed a division between them. Those from the North, or Trouvères, sang of chivalrous histories, such as those of Charlemagne, of Arthur and the Round Table; while those from the South sang of love, of chivalry, joustings, and so forth. From want of space I cannot go deeper just now into the subject, but I will just mention that the spirit of these two kinds of ballads have been curiously preserved to us by two poets, who can hardly be said to belong to the Troubadours. Petrarch may be said to have been the Troubadour of Italy, which country had properly none else of its own, though he came a century later than the true Troubadours. I refer to his great genius in sonnets and love singing. In him was a refined spirit of the Troubadour poetry; doubtless it had many faults, but there it is in its more complete shape, as it lay in the melodious mind of Petrarch. This kind of song was cultivated even by kings and princes, such as Richard Cœur de Lion and Barbarossa.

The other production to which I have alluded, of the Troubadour school, is better known by the name of the Niebelungen Lied. This is properly Trouvère. The probable date of this poem is the twelfth century; it is by far the finest poem connected with the Middle Ages, down to Dante. It is of the old heroic German spirit, and sounds true as steel. It commemorates the adventures of the early

Chiefs, of Siegfried and King Attila, and of the whole nation from their emigrations downwards, all shadowed out there. It is of the first rate, not perhaps evincing a shining genius, but far better than that, the simple, noble, manly character of its age, full of religion, mercy, and valour! It was discovered about sixty years ago, but became generally known only forty years after that. I advise any of my friends who know German to make this poem their study; a modern German translation of it has been published, but the language of the original is not much older to the German scholar than Chaucer is to us, and it is by far the finest poem we have of that period.

We must now quit this general investigation of the Middle Ages, but I must, in the last place, remark that we must not suppose because the spirit of those ages did not *speak* much it has been lost, or ever could have been lost. It is not so ordered. There is no good action man can do that is not summoned up in time to come, and kept up there. We lose, indeed, much of the inconsistencies and contradictions of the times in the lapse of ages. But this again is precisely what we observe of rude natural voices, heard singing in the distance. Musicians say that there is nothing so strikingly impressive as to hear a psalm, for instance, sung by untaught voices in the mountains; many inaccuracies, no doubt, there are in the performance, but in the distance all is true and bright, because all false notes destroy one another, and are absorbed in the air before they reach us, and only the true notes come to us. So in the Middle Ages we only get the heroic essence of the whole. Actions only will be found to have been preserved when writers are forgotten. Homer will one day be swallowed up in time, and so will all the greatest writers that have ever lived, and comparatively this is very little matter. But actions will not be destroyed, their influence must live; good or bad they will live throughout eternity, **for the** weal or woe of the doer! In particular, the good actions will flow on, in the course of time unseen perhaps, but just as a river of **water** flowing underground, hidden in general, but at intervals breaking out to the surface in many a well for the refreshment of men!

In **our next** lecture we shall come to Dante.

LECTURE V.

May 14th.

SECOND PERIOD—*continued.*

DANTE—THE ITALIANS—CATHOLICISM—PURGATORY.

We are now arrived at that **point of history** when Europe becomes divided; its great **stem** branches off into different nations, one nation forming itself after another. Each nation of modern Europe distinguishes itself in some measure from all other nations. The language is the peculiar product of each nation, containing something of its own not supplied from the others; the function so appointed to be done by it, and the genius of it, everything belonging to it, characterises each nation. We shall take them in their order.

The first nation which possesses a claim **on** our solicitude is the Italian. It was the latest nation of those overrun by the barbarians which fashioned itself into something of an articulate result. It has much distinguished itself in Europe, in ancient, as well as in modern times. It was the first that was notable in literature, in the exposition of opinions, in arts, in all the products of the human intellect. It is also important from being connected with that characteristic of the Middle Ages, the religious feeling then prevalent. It was the latest settled, and the first notable; it was the last modern nation where the tumult of the northern emigrations subsided. The Lombards conquered Italy in the sixth century; they were the latest of the German tribes that left their native seat. Paul Diaconus wrote their history. The Lombards, or Longobardi (Longbeards), were a brave, gifted, excellent nation; they ruled in Italy for 150 years, after which time it split itself into a number of small principalities and towns, and so it has unhappily continued ever since. The next memorable event is the conquest of the South of Italy by the Guiscards, in the eleventh century, some two or three centuries after the final decay of the Lombard power. They were the sons of Tancred de Hauteville, the most impetuous fighters Italy ever had to encounter. The part where they settled was that which was remarked to have been once colonised by Greeks, Magna Græcia, where to this day many Greek usages are still preserved. Part of it is now called Naples (Neapolis, new town). The Saracens had gained a footing there, and to dislodge them the Prince of Apulia sent for Guiscard. He and his brother, who was called Iron Arm, came over and eventually repelled the Saracens. It was a great thing to do: it was not much more than 100 years after these Normans (Northmen) had emerged from the condition of wild pirates, and settled in France, which was also about 100 years before the time of William the Conqueror.

It was a great feat. Naples was rendered a dependency of Northern Europe, and has remained so ever since.

If it had not been for the third memorable circumstance respecting Italy, the existence in it of the Pope, an event not sudden but gradual (1077 was the culminating age of this political power), the Guiscards would have conquered all Italy. But the Pope had by this time got settled, and had territories of his own. He did not choose to permit the Guiscards to make further encroachments; accordingly, he interdicted their progress, and thus doomed Italy to be for ever divided, and, politically speaking, entirely paralysed. If the Pope or the Guiscards, no matter which, had got ground throughout Italy, the result would have been very happy for her, but it was not her lot. Lingering still there in Italy, we observe that she occupies very little place in Europe; but Italy has a peculiar character, and though Italians complain that their country has not held that influence in modern Europe to which, from her position and resources, she is entitled, still I do not think that we should say that her part has not been a great one. In one respect it has been much greater than that of any other nation. She has produced a far greater number of great men, distinguished in art, thinking, conduct, and everywhere in the departments of intellect. Dante, Raphael, Michael Angelo, among others, are hardly to be paralleled, in the respective department of each of these. In other departments again, there are Columbus, Spinola, and Galileo. And, after all, the great thing which any nation can do is to produce great men. It is thus only that it distinguishes itself in reality, and this distinction lasts longer than any other. A battle would be a comparatively trivial and poor thing!

In our limits it is impossible to attempt the delineation of the Italian people; but in every people there is to be found some one great product of intellect, and when we shall have explained the significance of that one, we shall not fail to understand all the rest. In this instance we shall take Dante, one of the greatest men that ever lived; perhaps the very greatest of Italians, certainly one of the greatest. The *Divina Commedia* is Dante's work. He was from Florence, a town of all others fertile in great men; he was born in 1265. Florence had already come into note 200 years before that; it was first founded by Sylla. In the Middle Ages it played a great part, and it was there that Dante was born. His family was one of the greatest in Florence, that of Durante Alighieri (Durante since corrupted to Dante). He was well educated. We hear mention made of the schoolmaster who taught him grammar, and other great men of the day who had to do with him in different branches of education. He was much occupied in public employments in his native town. Twice he was engaged in battle, on one occasion with the Republic of Pisa, and he was employed in fourteen embassies. It was in his twenty-fifth year that he first fought for Florence—in the battle of Arezzo, I think; and finally he became Prior or chief magistrate of Florence.

We can make nothing of those obscure quarrels. They have no interest for us—those quarrels of the Guelphs and Ghibellines. We saw the foundation of all that in the quarrel of Hildebrand with the Emperor. Year after year it went on, generation after generation. The people that favoured the Pope were called Guelphs; those who favoured the Emperor, Ghibellines. The Guelphs were German princes. The Ghibellines were so named from Weiblin, a town of the Hohenstaufen, near Weinsberg. Their real names were Welf and Weiblin. Weiblin was made by the Italians into Ghibelline. The Guelphs were the ancestors of the house of Brunswick, the family on the throne of these realms. I say that we can make nothing out of these quarrels, except that in every town of Italy party hatred prevailed violently, and each faction directed its utmost endeavours to supplant the other.

Dante favoured the side of the Emperor. There being a very small number of families in Florence, party hatred was proportionally more violent. Banishments of the highest personages were quite common there, and were employed as often as one party was trodden down by its enemies. Dante accordingly, being then absent upon some embassy, was banished by his enemies. He was then in his thirty-fifth year. He afterwards made some attempt, with others of his friends, to get back to Florence, and made an attack by arms upon the city, which, proving unsuccessful, so exasperated the citizens that nothing could appease them. Dante was then as good as confiscated; he had been fined before that. There is still to be seen an act of that time in the archives of Florence, charging all magistrates to burn Dante alive when he should be taken, such violent hatred had they conceived against him! Dante was afterwards reduced to wander up and down Italy, a broken man! His way of life is difficult to conceive of, with so violent a mind as his, with such deep feelings, whether sad or joyful. Henceforth he had sorrow for his portion. It is very mournful to think of, but, at the same time, the work he had to do could not have been done so well had his lot been less unhappy. He was ever a serious man, always meditating on some religious or moral subject. After his misfortunes, besides, there was no hope extant for him; he tells us that he had left everything he could love. This gave him double and treble earnestness of character. The world was now all over for him; he looked now only to the great kingdom of eternity! It has been disputed whether he had begun the *Divina Commedia* before he left Florence. He had, at all events, not written much of it. He completed it in his exile, that he might secure to himself powerful friends, who could shelter him; and he therefore got it published, to be descanted on now 500 years after that, and to continue to be so for 1000 years and more to come!

There are few things that exist worth comparing to it. Æschylus, Dante, Shakespeare—one really cannot add another greater name to these! Theirs were the utterances out of the great heart of nature, sincere outpourings of the mind of man! His *Divina Commedia* assumes at first the form of a vision, though it soon loses it as he proceeds. Indeed, he nowhere expressly announces it at all, though he begins suddenly, as if it were a vision. The three great kingdoms of Eternity are the subject of the poem: Hell, the place of final expiation of guilt, where a stern, inexorable justice reigns without pity, charged to inflict punishments for infraction of the laws of the Most High; Purgatory, a place where the sin of man is, under certain conditions, cleansed away; and Paradise, where the soul enjoys felicity for ever! This was the greatest idea that we have ever yet had—the experience of entering into the soul of man, more full of grandeur than any other of the elements, and it fell to the lot of one who was singularly appropriated by his way of life for the task. He was a man full of sorrows, a man of woe; by nature of a serious turn of mind, and rendered doubly and trebly so by his way of life. Accordingly, I think that when all records of Catholicism shall have passed away; when the Vatican shall have crumbled into dust, and St. Peter's and Strasburg Minster be no more; for thousands of years to come Catholicism will survive in this sublime relic of antiquity!

In seeking the character of Dante's poem, we shall admire first that grand natural, moral depth, that nobleness of heart, that grandeur of soul which distinguish him. Great in all directions, in his wrath, his scorn, his pity. Great above all in his sorrow! That is a fine thing which he says of those in a state of despair, 'They have not the Hope to die'—'*Non hanno speranza di morte!*' What an idea that is in Dante's mind there of death. To most persons death is the dreaded being, the king of terrors, but to Dante to be imprisoned for ever in a miserable complexity, without hope of release, is the most terrible of things! Indeed, I believe, notwithstanding the horror of death, no human creature but would find it to be the most dreadful doom not to be suffered to die, though he should be decreed to enjoy all youth and bloom immortally! For there is a boundlessness, an endless longing, in the breast, which aspires to another world than this.

That, too, is a striking passage where he says of certain individuals that they are hateful to God, and to the enemies of God. There was a deep feeling in Dante of the enormity of that moral baseness, such as had never before gone into the mind of any man. These of whom he speaks were a kind of trimmers; men that had not even the merit to join with the devil. He adds: '*Non ragioniam di lor, ma guarda e passa!*'—'Let us say nothing of them, but look and pass!' The central quality of Dante was greatness of heart; from this all the others flowed as from a natural source. This must exist in every man that would be great; it is impossible for him to do anything good without it, and by his success we may trace, in every writer, his magnanimity and his pusillanimity. In Dante there was the greatness of simplicity, for one thing. All things are to be anticipated from the nobleness of his moral opinions. Logically speaking, again, Dante had one of the finest understandings, remarkable in all matters of reason; as, for instance, in his reflections on fortune, free-will, and the nature of sin. He was an original, quick, far-seeing man, possessing a deep insight into all matters, and this, combined with the other quality which we noticed, his greatness of heart, constitutes the principal charm in Dante. In the third place, his poem was so musical that it got up to the length of singing itself, his soul was in it; and when we read there is a tune which hurries itself along. These qualities, a great heart, insight, and song, are the stamp of a genuine poem at all times. They will not be peculiar to any one age, but will be natural in all ages. For, as I observed, it is the utterance of the heart of life itself, and all earnest men, of whatever age, will there behold as in a mirror the image of their own convexed beam, and will be grateful to the poet for the brotherhood to him in which they stand. Then as to simplicity, there is in the poem throughout that noble character, insomuch that one would almost suppose that there is nothing great there. For he remains intent upon the delineation of his subject, never guilty of bombastic inflation, and does not seem to think that he is doing anything very remarkable. Herein he is very different from Milton. Milton, with all his genius, **was very** inferior to Dante, he has made his angels large, huge, distorted beings. He has sketched vividly his scenes of heaven and **hell, and his** faculty is certainly great; but I say that Dante's **task** was the great thing to do. He has opened the deep, unfathomable oasis of woe that lay in the soul of man; he has opened the living fountains of hope, also of penitence! And this I say is far greater than towering as high as Teneriffe, or twice as high!

In his delineations he has a most beautiful sharp grace, the quickest and clearest intellect. It is just that honesty with which his mind was set upon his subject, that carries it out. Take, for instance, **the scene** of the monster Geryon, with Virgil and **Dante**, where he describes how he landed with them **in** the eighth **circle.** He says **that** Geryon **was** like a falcon in quest of prey, hovering without seeing either the lure or the game. When the falconer cries, '*Oimè tu cali*' ('Come down!'), he descends, wheeling round and round, and sits at a distance disdainful and disobedient. Just so was Geryon. And then he bolted up like an arrow out of the bow. There are **not** above a dozen words in this picture, but it is one that will **last** for ever!

So also his description of the city of Dis, to which Virgil **carries** him, possesses a beautiful simplicity and honesty. 'The light was so dim that the people could hardly see, and they winked at him, just as people wink their eyes under the new moon,' or as an old tailor winks threading his needle, when his eyes are not good. There is a contrast between his subject and this quaint similitude that has a beautiful effect. It brings one home to the subject; there is much reality in this similitude. So his description of the place they were in. Flakes of fire came down like snow, falling on the skin of the people, and burning them black! Among these he sees his old schoolmaster who taught him grammar, he winks at him in the manner described, but he is so burnt that Dante can hardly recognise him.

There are many of his greatest qualities in the celebrated passage about Francesca, whom he finds in the circle of Inferno appropriated to those who had erred in love. I many times say I know nowhere of a more striking passage; if any one would select a passage characteristic of a great man, let him study that. It is as tender as the voice of mothers, full of the gentlest pity, though there is much stern tragedy in it. It is very touching. In a place without light, which groaned like a stormy sea, he sees two shadows which he wishes to speak to, and they come to him. He compares them to doves whose wings are open and not fluttering. Francesca, one of these, utters her complaint, which does not occupy twenty lines, though it is such an one that a man may write a thousand lines about it, and not do ill. It contains beautiful touches of human weakness. She feels that stern justice encircles her all around. 'Oh, living creature,' she says, 'who hast come so kindly to visit us, if the Creator of the World' (poor Francesca! she knew that she had sinned against His inexorable justice) 'were our friend, we would pray Him for thy peace!' Love, which soon teaches itself to a gentle heart, inspired her Paolo (beautiful womanly feeling that). 'Love forbids that the person loved shall not love in return.' And so she loved Paolo. 'Caina awaits him who destroyed our life,' she adds with female vehemence. Then, in three lines, she tells the story how they fell in love. 'We read one day of Launcelot, how love possessed him; we were alone, we regarded one another; when we read of that laughing kiss, he, trembling, kissed me! That day,' she adds, 'we read no further!'

The whole is beautiful, like a clear, piping voice heard in the middle of a whirlwind: it is so sweet, and gentle, and good!

Then the hunger power of Ugolino. This, however, is a much more brutal thing than the punishment of Francesca. But the story of Francesca is all a truth. He says that he knew her father; her history becomes a kind of concern in the mind of Dante, and when he hears her relate it he falls as a dead body falls. This, too, is an answer to a criticism against Dante, and a paltry criticism it is. Some have regarded the poem as a kind of satire upon his enemies, on whom he revenged himself by putting them into hell. Now, nothing is more unworthy of Dante than such a theory. If he had been of such an ignoble nature, he never could have written the *Divina Commedia*. It was written in the purest spirit of justice. Thus he pitied poor Francesca, and would not have willingly placed her in that torment; but it was the justice of God's law that doomed her there!

How beautiful is his description of the coming eve, the hour when sorrow awakens in the hearts of sailors who have left their land (*squilla di lontano*), the dying day. No one ever quitted home and loved ones whose heart does not respond to that!

We must not omit Farinata, the beautiful illustration of a character much found in Dante. He is confined in the black dome where the heretics dwell. In the same tomb is Cavalcante de' Cavalcanti, father of one of Dante's most loved friends. The description is striking of the sarcophaguses in which these people are enclosed, 'more or less heated' (there is nothing in Teneriffe like that); the lids are to be kept open till the last day, and are then to be sealed down for ever. He hears Dante speaking in the Tuscan dialect, and he accosts him. He is a man of great haughtiness (*gran dispitto, sdegnoso*). This spirit of defiance of suffering, so remarkable in Æschylus, occurs two or three times in Dante. Farinata asks him, What news of Florence? For in all his long exile Dante himself thinks continually of Florence, which he loves so well, and he makes even those in torment anxious after what is doing in Florence. Then Cavalcanti asks Dante why is he there, and not his son. Where is he? And Dante replies that perhaps he had disdain for Virgil. *Had?* Cavalcanti asks (*Ebbe*); does he not live then? And, as Dante pauses a little without replying, he plunges down, **and Dante sees him no more!**

These sudden and abrupt motions are frequent in Dante. **He** is, indeed, full of what I can call military movements; many of his gestures are extremely significant. In another place three men 'looked at one another, like men that believed.' In these words one sees it all, as it seemed to Dante! This **is** a feature I don't know how to name well, but it is very remarkable in Dante. Those passages are very striking where he alludes to his own sad fortunes. There is in them a wild sorrow, a savage tone of truth, a breaking heart; the hatred **of** Florence, **and with it** the love of Florence! In one place, 'Rejoice, O Florence, that thou **art so** famous in hell!' In another place he calls her hell-guided. His old schoolmaster tells him: 'If thou follow thy star, thou canst not miss a happy harbour.' That was just it. That star occasionally shone on him from the blue eternal depths, and he felt he was doing something good; but he soon lost it again as he fell back into the trough of the sea, and had to journey on as before. And when his ancestor predicts his banishment, there is the wild sincerity again. He must leave every delightful thing; he must learn **to dwell on** the stairs of another man. **Bitter! bitter!** Poor exile, **none** but scoundrelly persons to associate with! There are traces here and there of a heart one would always wish to see in man. He is not altogether, therefore, an unconscious man like Shakespeare, but more morbid and narrower. Though he does not attempt to compute it, he seems to feel merely the conviction, the humble hope, that he shall get to heaven in the end!

A notable passage that on fame! No man, if he were Alexander the Great, if he were Dante, if he were all men put together, could get for himself eternal fame! He feels that, too. Fame is not of any particular moment to him. That contradiction between the greatness of his mind and his humble attachment to Florence is difficult of utterance, and it seems as if the spirit of the man were hampered with the insufficient dialects this world imposes upon him.

The 'Inferno' has become of late times mainly the favourite of the three divisions of Dante's great poem. It has harmonised well with the taste of the last thirty or forty years, in which Europe has seemed to covet more a violence of emotion and a strength of convulsion than almost any other quality. It is no doubt a great thing; but to my mind the 'Purgatorio' is excellent also, and I question even whether it is not a better and a greater thing on the whole. It is very beautiful to see them get up into that black, great mountain in the western ocean, where Columbus had not yet been. To trace *giro* after *giro*, the purification of souls is beautiful exceedingly; the sinners' repentance, the humble hope, the peace and joy that is in them.

There is no book so moral as this, the very essence of Christian morality! Men have, of course, ceased to believe these things—that mountain rising up in the ocean, or that Male-bolge, with its black gulfs. But still men of any knowledge at all must believe that there exists the inexorable justice of God, and that penitence is the great thing here for man. For life is but a series of errors, made good again by repentance; and the sacredness of that doctrine is asserted in Dante in a manner more moral than anywhere else. Any other doctrine is with him comparatively not worth affirming or denying. Very touching is that gentle patience, that unspeakable thankfulness with which the souls expect their release after thousands of years. Cato is keeping the gate. That is a beautiful dawn of morning. The dawn drove away the darkness westward, with a quivering of the sea on the horizon.

'Si che di lontano
Conobbi al tremolar della marina.'

He seems to seize the word for it. Anybody who has seen the sun rise at sea will recognise it. The internal feeling of the 'Purgatorio' keeps pace with that. One man says: 'Tell my Giovanna that I think her mother does not love me now'— that she has laid aside her weeds! The parable with which he concludes his lament is as beautiful as it can be.

Then, too, the relation he stands in to Virgil and Beatrice; his loyalty, faith, and kindly feeling for Virgil's nobleness. Loyalty, we remarked, was the essence of the Middle Ages. Virgil was never angry with him but once, when Dante seems to pay too much attention to two falsifiers quarrelling. 'A little more,' he says, 'and I would quarrel with thee.' Dante owns himself in the wrong, and Virgil then tells him it is not proper to listen to such things. Beatrice was actually a beautiful little girl, whom he had seen in his boyhood at a ball. She was a young child, nine years old when he was ten. He had never heard her speak but once, when she was talking to some one at the corner of the street. She was cinctured with a garland of olive, and appeared '*miræ pulchritudinis.*' Such was the mood of beauty, he says, in which her aspect placed him, that that night, when he fell asleep, he dreamed of her. This was at nine o'clock, for though it was many years after he remembered it quite well. They had met but little, but he seemed to know that she loved him, as he her. She married another afterwards, but not willingly. When all else is dark with misery for him, this is the only recollection that is beautiful, for nothing had occurred to render it disagreeable to him, and his whole soul flies to it. Providence sent an angel always to interfere when the worst came. In Paradise, when Virgil vanishes and he sees Beatrice, by this time purified from mortal stain, how deep is the expression of his joy!

How heavily the love he bore her weighed upon his heart! The mother of Beatrice treated him with much seeming harshness (*barbarezza*), wasting his very life away with severity; but it was all through her apprehension that if she were to give vent to her love for him she should kill him; it would be too much for him. But he reads in her eye all the while her deep affection; in the flush of joy with which she regards him, his successes, and good actions. One can well understand, in this point of view, what the Germans say of the three parts of the *Divina Commedia*. The first is the architectural, plastic part, as of statuary; the second is the pictorial; the third is the musical, the melting into song.

But I can afford no more time to speak of Dante. My friends must endeavour to supply the omissions I have been obliged to make, and to expand what I have said over his whole poem. We must quit Italy and Dante altogether with these imperfect remarks.

LECTURE VI.

May 18th.

SECOND PERIOD—*continued.*

THE SPANIARDS — CHIVALRY — GREATNESS OF THE SPANISH NATION — CERVANTES, HIS LIFE, HIS BOOK — LOPE — CALDERON — PROTESTANTISM AND THE DUTCH WAR.

IN our last lecture we saw the remarkable phenomenon of one great mind making of himself, as it were, the spokesman of his age, and speaking with such an earnestness and depth that he has become one of the voices of mankind itself, making his voice to be heard in all ages, for he was filled in every fibre of his mind with that principle, belief in the Catholic Church: this was the model by which all things became satisfactorily arranged for him in his mind. We must now leave that altogether abruptly, and come to the next great phenomenon in this history, a new nation, new products in the human mind. I allude to Cervantes and chivalry. But before I come to that I may observe that Dante's way of thinking was one which from its very nature could not long continue; indeed, it is not given to man that any of his works should long continue, of the works of his mind, any more than the things which he makes with his hand. But there was something in the very nature of Dante's way of thinking which made it very natural that it should have become generally altered even in the next generation. Dante's son even must have lived in an increased horizon of knowledge, which the theory of Dante could no longer fit; as, for example, man had then sailed to the Western Ocean, and had found that the Mountain of Purgatory was not there at all. Indeed, if we look at it, we shall find that every man is first a learner, an apprentice, and then a workman, who at first schemes out to himself such knowledge as his fathers teach him into quite a familiar theory; but the first researches will further widen his circle of knowledge, and he will have certain misgivings as to the theory, the creed I may call it, of the universe which he has already adopted, certain suspicions in his own mind that there are inconsistencies and contradictions in his theory not at all satisfactory, and this will go on increasing until this theory alters itself, shapes itself to them.

In Italy the same Catholic Church, which was the mother of the mind of Dante, inspiring it with every feeling and thought that was there, afterwards condemned Galileo to renounce what he knew to be true because it was at that time supposed to be contrary to the tenets the Church held on the subject, forcing him to be either the martyr of the

Inquisition or to deny the truth. Indeed, before that, Europe had split itself into all kinds of confusions and contradictions without end, in which we are still enveloped. This, in short, is the foundation and essence of the progress of the human mind,— which, in spite of the exaggerations and the misrepresentations which have been made of it, is really the inevitable law for man, to go on, and to continue to widen his investigations for thousands of years, or even for millions, for there is no limit to it! Any theory of Nature is, at most, temporary; but, on the other hand, all theories contain something within them which is perennial. In Dante that was belief, the communion which the heart of hearts can hold with Nature. The human soul, in fact, develops itself into all sorts of opinions, doctrines which go on nearer and nearer to the truth. All theories approximate more or less to the great Theory, which remains itself always unknown, and in that proportion contain something which must live. Therefore, whatever opinion we may form of his doctrines, we do not dissent from Dante's piety, that will always be admired. There is no nation, too, without progress. Some people say that the Chinese are without it; perhaps they may change less rapidly than other nations, but they *must* change. It appears to me to be inevitably necessary. Every philosophy that exists is destined to be embraced, melted down as it were, into some larger philosophy, which, too, will have to suffer the same some day.

Cervantes lived more than two centuries after Dante; though we select him as the most remarkable of his age there were, no doubt, before him many other people very valuable in influencing the human mind. All people, indeed, from Charlemagne's time, had already made rapid advances in all departments of culture. We may here remark one or two symptoms of that restless effort after advancement then in action everywhere in Europe. First there was the institution of universities, which was long before Dante. The University of Paris had come into decided note in the time of Dante. There is a tradition that Dante himself was at it, as there is a vague tradition that he was at Oxford too, but this last is very doubtful. These universities of Europe grew up in a very obscure manner, not noted at first, but rising up quite naturally and spontaneously. Some great teacher, such as Abelard, would get into repute with those who were eagerly desirous of learning, and there would be no other way of learning his knowledge except to gather round him and hear him expound what knowledge he had in his own department. When any other teacher would be desirous of displaying his own branch of acquirements he would naturally establish himself in the neighbourhood of the first one, and so these many teachers would begin to gather themselves together till their community should become known generally, and more young men would resort to them, until finally the king, as did the King of France, would take notice of them, form them into a corporation, endow them with lands, and style the establishment university—the place of a complete, settled course of instruction. It was about the ninth century that Paris was first recognised as an university, others soon followed, and the system so founded continues down to our times. One cause may be assigned for their existence, the want of books.

Books at that period were not easily to be procured, and except by means of lecturing none could learn what knowledge there was then to be attained. But this want became supplied by another great symptom of European improvement, the invention of the art of printing in the century after Dante, that is to say, the end of the fifteenth and beginning of the sixteenth centuries. There are many controversies as to where it was invented, but it is not necessary to examine them here. Fust brought it into full use about the year 1450. It is one very great fact productive of important results for mankind, and one which has not clearly unfolded itself yet; but it was by no means a wonderful invention, it was quite a corollary from another great art, writing, a much more wonderful achievement, yet comparatively insignificant too, compared with that admirable gift of speech, that power which man has of expressing his meaning by certain sounds!

Another symptom of the change of habits in Europe is the invention of gunpowder, which took place prior to the century before the invention of printing, two centuries we may say; but the time of this invention is not known either; also some attribute it to Friar Bacon, and others to Swartz. It does not seem a very beneficent invention this, designed for the destruction of man; but yet, on the whole, it has had immense consequences of the beneficial sort, for, like all other things in military art, it softens the miseries of war, and, we may add, without entering into any wide conclusions about it, it is really the setting of the soul of man above the body of man, since it has reduced physical strength all to nothing in the contests between man and man, insomuch that, give the weakest woman a pistol, and she instantly becomes a Goliath with that pistol in her hand! A great invention that; so busy were these ages in their efforts after progress!

We shall now proceed to look at the Spaniards, and the results they realised for themselves in this world of ours. The two great things which we have remarked in the Middle Ages—first, Christianity: the Catholic religion; and next, loyalty—had mainly the influence over Dante's works. That same spirit of loyalty obtained, however, a practical illustration of a striking character, which received the name of Chivalry. This, we may say, was the great product of the Spanish nation. It seems very extraordinary that Christianity, which is against war altogether, teaching men even not to resist violence, should, with its divine spirit, have penetrated even into war itself, making it in the highest degree noble and beneficial; that that dark background which lies in every man, and which tells him that he can fight, and makes war at all times possible for man, that even this should have been penetrated with that spirit, and raised by it to an elevation, a nobleness, a beauty quite distinguished from anything in the pagan world!

The age of chivalry has been the subject of all kinds of investigations, but writers have been able to find no physical origin for it. It seems to have been produced by the German spirit united to that of the Christian doctrine. Among the Germans courage in battle was greatly honoured. According to Tacitus, when a young man aspired to manhood, he was solemnly led into the Public Assembly, there girt with a sword, and proclaimed a fighter and a man.

This is very analogous to the ceremonies of knighthood, chivalry. This German quality, valour of character, combined with the Christian religion, as well as with another feature of the Germans, their reverence for women, which also became a feature of chivalry. These two qualities of the German character became blended under the sanctifying influence of Christianity, and the whole framed itself into a system of opinions of the most beneficial kind, tempering the horrid madness of war, man meeting to kill man, and presenting a most beautiful glow of worth, very different from what war was in old times, where indeed there were always certain laws of war (as what can be done without some law or other at any time), but there was none of that mercy, that noble self-denial, that fidelity to a man, and to the **cause** of that man, which we see in the Middle Ages!

In the next place, **I** may observe that probably the Spanish nation was the most fitted for this matter, **as** it **actually** appears to have carried this matter forward to a higher perfection than it attained anywhere else. The Spanish nation had made its appearance in European history more than two centuries before Christ, in the wars of the **Carthaginians** and **Romans**. They were remarkable for their tenacious valour. The Celt-iberian nation, the origin of the rest of Spain, had always that character, and to this day they maintain it in Spain by the name of Basques, and on the other side of **the Pyrenees by that of** Gascons. In the barbarian invasions they at first became mixed with the Goths, **and** afterwards with the Vandals, from whom they received their slight admixture of Northern blood; and then with the Arabs. In modern times they maintained the nobleness which distinguished them in ancient times, and have often displayed a spirit equal to that they exhibited in the sieges of Saguntium and Numantia, which lasted fourteen years, and the scenes of which are much analagous to the siege of Saragossa in our times: a striking instance which shows the character of nations to be wonderfully **tenacious. The Spaniards** had less breadth of genius than the Italians, but they had, on the other hand, **a lofty** sustained enthusiasm in a higher degree than the Italians, with a tinge of what we call romance, a dash of Oriental exaggeration, and a tenacious vigour in prosecuting their objects. Of less depth than the Germans, of less of that composed silent force, yet a great people, and of much knowledge, and at all times calculated to be distinguished; and it was this people that developed the thing we call chivalry: that system of noble deeds in war, and noble feelings. These sieges of Saguntium and Numantia, and the man Viriatus, a Spanish or Portuguese shepherd, who withstood the whole force of the Romans for fourteen years—that same spirit which was in them showed itself early in modern Europe, in the Cid, for example—whose memory is still musical among the people. I am told that to this day they sing ballads about him. A book has been written about his history by Johannes von Müller, who really sees good reason to give credit to the popular ballads about his adventures. You all know the famous version of it by Corneille. His real name was Ruy Diaz. He was the contemporary of William the Conqueror; from the first a hard destiny was laid out for him. He had been betrothed to Lady Chimene, but their fathers disagreeing, the match was broken off; a contest ensued, in which his father was vanquished. For the purpose of vengeance, he fought and conquered her father, merely from a sentiment of filial duty, not from interest; all personal wishes were set at nought, and as to thoughts of personal advantage, it was altogether the reverse. So when the King had employed him successfully against the Moors, he afterwards rejected him altogether from his Court. He fought often against the Moors. (I may here mention that Cid is a Moorish name, and signifies master.) No doubt those contests against the Arabs tended very much to keep alive that spirit of chivalry. This people first landed in Spain in the eighth century, and very soon overran it, and even penetrated into France as far as Poitou, where they were met by Charles Martel, and driven back upon Spain. We may say that they made themselves masters of all Spain. The Christian people took refuge in the mountains, and, issuing from thence, gradually reconquered the country; but that contest lasted 800 years. Notwithstanding their hostility, we must confess the Moors did great things for Spain. They—invented the decimal system of notation, the greatest boon the world perhaps ever got in that department; also they gave us the words azimuth, nadir, zenith—in all sciences they effected great results. They were the first who translated the Greek books; and, in short, were the instructors of Europe in many respects. But in particular, we are to remark of them that they serve especially to illustrate what was said of the Middle Ages, and the effect of belief at that time.

The nation, ever since the time of their probable founders (Hagar and Ishmael), had been a nation of great energy, but living alone in their deserts, and entirely obscure in that way of life, until Mahomet, the Prophet of Arabia, appeared. This was in the seventh century. I must say that I regard this man as no impostor at all, and I am glad to think so for the honour of our human nature, but, as an enthusiastic man, who had by the powers of his own mind gained a flash of the truth, living a quiet simple life till the age of forty, then striking out into a new path altogether, deeply impressed with the heinousness of Arabian idolatry, and full of the great truth, that God was one; in other respects a poor inferior mortal, full of sensuality, corruption, and ignorance, as he showed by the rewards he promised the Arabs when he spoke out his system to them. He got them, but with much difficulty, to believe that, and then within a century afterwards they had spread themselves, like gunpowder ignited by a spark, across the Indies on the one hand, and on the other up as far as Poitou! They made, besides, great proficiency in the arts, poetry, science, and were greatly superior in all these respects to any European nation of the time.

In Cervantes we see almost the first record of Spanish literature. Viriatus, the Cid, and the like men lived silent; their works spoke for them, and it is singular that a poor obscure man should be the only voice which has reached us through so many ages of Spanish history, without which, too, we should never have so accurately known what was the tone of the Spanish soul. His life was not that of a scholar at all, but of a broken, active, hard man of action. He was of a decayed family of gentry of Ascalon, near Madrid; his birth took place in 1547. Being placed at school, he soon distinguished himself, insomuch that he was able to obtain an employment under the Cardinal Aquaviva, who was then going to Rome; but the great league being about that time formed between Rome, Spain, and Venice against the Turks, he resigned his post, and became a soldier, as did many young men and noblemen then, volunteering to serve in the fleet under Colonna and Don John of Austria. The battle of Lepanto was the beginning of his hard experience; there his left arm was cut off by a Turkish scimitar. Returning home to Spain, though he had not quitted the army notwithstanding his wound, he was taken captive by a Barbary corsair, carried to Algiers, and there compelled to dig the ground in the service of the rude and cruel corsair, his master. Seven years he spent in slavery and the most grievous suffering; but his cheerful and noble heart kept him up. He spent the whole of this time in devising means to get out of the place.

In Don Quixote he has given us the story of a captive's adventures, distinctly resembling his own. Besides this, in a book upon Barbary, written by a Spanish priest in the same century, the author, Father Haydo, gives an account of Cervantes' captivity and adventures, of his plans of escape; that he and others lived in a cavern for six months, hoping to get away; that he escaped death many times, and in particular on the occasion of his escape into the cavern, where he was detected; that he was there very nearly killed, and would have been had not the Dey of Algiers consented to let him ransom himself for 500 crowns if he were able. His mother and sister and others then began to contribute towards this amount, as it was too much for one of them to bear; and it is very touching to see how one would give fifty crowns, and another perhaps not so much, and so on. But the Society of Mercy was then active in ransoming Christian slaves, and, among others, they were induced to ransom Cervantes. He was then in his **thirty-fourth** year. He married shortly after; but he made at that time no progress in literature. He was taken up by some of his kindred about Seville, who were merchants there, and in their employment he occupied himself by travelling up and down Spain, which, by these means, he came to know accurately, and could not have known so well in **any other** way.

He finally came to Valladolid to settle, but it is not known why he did so. There is yet a curious document in the archives of Valladolid, which shows his humble condition and the small **estimation in** which he was then held. A man, it appears from this record, was one night murdered in front of Cervantes' house. Cervantes ran out to give assistance upon hearing the cry, but, being found with the corpse, he was taken up by the police, and carried away from his family before the magistrates. His house was so mean, where he and his family lived on the fourth floor, **and** their appearance was so haggard and squalid, that he was suspected of being one of the worst characters in the place. Of course he was cleared of this charge; but it is a striking record of the state of misery to which he was then reduced. Yet he was always, in spite of all this, as cheerful as any man could be; and the best proof of this is that that very year, some say before that, he produced the first part of Don Quixote, being then in his fifty-fourth year, already in old age. The last part appeared ten years after that, in the year before he died. It has been often remarked that he died on the same day that Shakespeare died. Some grandees and others gave him in his latter years some slight help, the Duke of Lemos, for example, for which he was abundantly grateful to them; but he was never lifted at any time above the state of poverty and dependence, and was always, as he said himself, the 'poorest of Spanish poets.' Three or four days, or perhaps two weeks, before his death, he writes to his patron, the Duke of Lemos, expressing warmly his gratitude for his favours to him, and taking leave of him, as he says, with his 'foot in the stirrup.' His had been a hard condition, full of privations and evils, necessity and difficulty. In none of his literary things he seems to prosper but Don Quixote, which, indeed, is a most admirable work; and it really seems as if Fortune, in return for her many unkindnesses, had given him this high gift—the power of speaking out the spirit that was in him in a way that should rank him among the great voices of the world.

Don Quixote is the very reverse of the *Commedia* of Dante; but in one respect it is analogous to it. Like it, it is the free utterance of the heart of man and nature. At the outset Cervantes seems to have contemplated not much more than a satire on chivalry—a burlesque. But, as he proceeds, the spirit soon grows on him. One may say that in his Don Quixote he pourtrays his own character, representing himself with good-natured irony, mistaking the illusions of his own heart for realities; but he proceeds ever more and more harmoniously. The first time where he appears to have gone deeply into his subject is the scene with the goatherds, where Don Quixote breaks out into an eulogy on the Golden Age, full of the finest poetry, although strangely introduced in the middle of the mockery which appears before. Throughout the delineation of the Don's character and the incidents of the story, there is the vesture of mockery, parody, with a seam of poetry shining through all; and above all we see the good-humoured cheerfulness of the author, in the middle of his unfortunate destiny; never provoked with it, no atrabiliar quality ever obtained any mastery in his mind! It was written in satire of the romances of chivalry; but it is the only record we have of many of them, and it is questionable whether any of those romances would have lasted till now if not noticed there. We have no time at all to dwell upon its merits. There is one thing, however, we should remark—that all the world seems to have a taste for the worth of it, and it is of all books the most universally read except the Bible.

Independently of chivalry, it is valuable, too, **as a** sort of sketch of the perpetual struggle in the human soul. We have the hard facts **of** this world's existence, and the ideal scheme struggling with these in a high enthusiastic manner delineated there; and for this there is no more wholesome vehicle anywhere than irony, the best way in which these ideas can live. If he had given us only a high-flown panegyric of the Age of Gold he would have found no ear for him, it is the self-mockery in which **he** envelopes it which reconciles us to the high bursts of enthusiasm, and which will keep the **matter alive** in the heart as long as there **are** men to read it! It is the poetry of comedy!

As a finish to all his noble qualities he possessed, in an eminent degree, the thing critics call humour, different from wit, mere laughter, which indeed seems to be much the same thing at first, though, in fact, widely different, and it has been said with much plausibility that the best test is, whether the writer in laughing at the objects of his wit, contemplates to produce an effect of any kind by it, or whether he is merely covering them with sport without **being contemplative of any such end; so that if any** one wishes to know the difference between humour and wit, the laughter of the fool, **which** the wise man, by a similitude founded on deep earnestness, called the crackling of thorns under a pot, let him read Cervantes on the one hand, and on the other, Voltaire, the greatest laugher the world ever knew.

There remain two other characters which (taking leave with great regret of Cervantes) I must now notice. One of these is Lope de Vega, and the other Calderon. Both contain a certain representation of the spirit of their age, although they do not come into actual contact with it. Of Calderon I have not read much, in fact, only one play and some choice specimens collected in German books, for his works are in great favour with the Germans, as much as the old dramas, Greek and others. They are extremely fond of Calderon, but I suspect that there is very much of *forced taste* in this; he did not strike me much, except for the wild, vague shape he gave to his characters. There is in general much of the mystic and vague in Calderon. No doubt he was a man of great earnestness of mind, and deep genius, and he was in his day more popular by far than Cervantes, also it is clear that his are the best Spanish plays. Of Lope de Vega I can say almost nothing, except that he too has obtained an historical name among us. A man of the strangest literary fortune! No man was ever so popular in his day as he was, courted by all, and even complimented in a letter by the Pope himself, insomuch that his name became proverbial for good fortune, or excellence, and it was the custom to call a fine day or

I

fine woman, a Lope day! a Lope woman! He certainly was a man of a strange facility, but of much shallowness too, and greatly inferior to Calderon; not that he was without genius, which if properly concentrated must have become productive of large results, but it was ill directed. He wrote one of his plays, he tells us, in twenty-four hours, and I believe he wrote above a hundred at the same rapid rate, so that he suffered his genius to be dissipated away in sound and vague splendour, and he has passed altogether out of our remembrance. He was certainly very successful in obtaining wages, yet he complains very much of them in a letter to his son, who had a great wish to learn literature, wherein he counselled him most earnestly not to think of such a thing, that the life of a literary man is full of bitterness and of poverty! This last was a singular complaint to come from him, as he certainly realised an immense sum of money by the profits of his works, and the presents that were made him. Still, he was a true poet in his way.

In the history of Spanish literature there are only these three, Cervantes, Calderon, and Lope, and Cervantes is far above the other two; and it is a curious reflection to make, that in so noble a nation, whose whole history is full of valiant actions and occurrences of every description, possessing so much cheerfulness, humanity, and quaint generosity, no writer for so many hundred years should have been produced who could speak the spirit of the nation, only Cervantes, an unknown, obscure individual, maimed, for he had lost an arm, and miserably poor. It is universally true that we cannot tell the meaning that is in men and things till a long time after their day. The Spanish nation was the most distinguished nation in the whole world. America was conquered by very great men of that nation; Cortes—Alexander the Great was not greater than Cortes! Pizarro, Balbo Nunez, the discoverer of the Pacific, of whom it is said that when he first beheld it he rushed into it till the waves reached his middle flourishing his sword, and took possession of the whole in the name of Spain with true chivalrous feeling; and, again, we see him patching up the roof of his hut with leaves, dressed in an old canvas jacket. They were the most enterprising people the world has seen yet. England and America, full as they are of the spirit of enterprise, do not carry us farther, and therefore I say that it is a strange and almost awful thing to consider how completely that nation has now passed away, sunk down into an insignificant and altogether mean nation. Many accounts have been attempted to be given for this, but even now one does not at all see why it should have so happened; we can only say just this, that its time was come, but the law which bound it cannot be understood at all!

It is curious to see how Spain broke itself to pieces in that conflict of Catholicism and chivalry with the Reformation, commonly called the Dutch

War. It is one of the most beautiful and heroic pieces of history to see a poor people, mere fishermen and shepherds, wishing to live quietly within their own dykes, and not to trouble the world at all, but who, happening to be among the first to receive a new doctrine, a new truth then preached in the world, could not get it maintained at all; but the Inquisition burned and branded them for it, and they were at last obliged to revolt in consequence against the then King of Spain, Philip II., and resisted him successfully during a thirty years' war. The result was what it always will be in such a struggle, the triumph of the right cause, of truth and justice over a system of downright falsehood and abomination. The siege of Leyden is a memorable event, it was surrounded by Spaniards on all sides, and reduced to the last straits by famine; but it was not yielded, the defenders declared that they were ready, if necessary, to eat their left arms, and fight on with the right. One day the poor people of the town met the Governor in his rounds, and told him that they must surrender, or they would die of hunger, but he told them not to speak of such a thing, to eat him if they chose, but not to surrender. In the end they succeeded, as we know, in cutting the dykes at Flushing, and letting out the water into the Spanish camp, which they attacked in the confusion, and thus delivered the city. Their resolution was inveterate: they wore, many of them, crescents in their caps, to show that they would be Turks rather than Papists.

This struggle lasted for thirty years, and first made the nation remarkable in the world ; the whole of it does great credit to the German people, to whom they belong.

This leads us naturally to the subject of our next lecture, 'The German People and the Reformation.'

LECTURE VII.

May 21st.

SECOND PERIOD—*(continued)*.

THE GERMANS—WHAT **THEY HAVE** DONE—REFORMATION—LUTHER—**ULRICH VON** HUTTEN—ERASMUS.

In our last lecture we had a glimpse of the Dutch War, the war between the Spanish and Dutch nations, and we observed the approach of a new life, the Reformation, and the Spanish Power wrecking itself against the Power it sought to molest, but which, instead, almost annihilated it. We are naturally led to look a little farther back into the causes of this new order of things, and to notice a new people more interesting to us, their descendants, than any we have yet noticed, namely, the Germans.

The German people has been mentioned in authentic records for the last 2100 years. The earliest notice we have of the Teutonic race is given in Luden's *History of Germany*, in a passage recovered from Pytheas, an obscure author mentioned by Strabo. This work of Pytheas, a sort of journal of a Marseilles merchant, in which he has noted down such observations as occurred to him in his commercial journeyings, mentions a people called Germans as a 'white-complexioned quiet people, living at the mouth of the Elbe.' What the Germans were before that, or what they had been doing from immemorial time, can never be known, but it is clear that they were a race of men designed for great things; perhaps even the highest of their destiny is not as yet attained. They became gradually known as they came into contact with the Romans; as the contact more and more increased, collision more and more increased, till at last the Empire itself was absorbed by them, and the dark anticipation of Tacitus realised: that one day Rome would be destroyed by these barbarians! In Tacitus' history, the old scanty records of German life are very interesting. Their character was certainly uncivilised, but not at all savage; it had a deep earnestness in it, and was that of a meditative people. The Scandinavian mythology is still a curious document, illustrative of many features of the German character. The account given of their form of worship by Tacitus evinces a very superior species of Paganism, indicative of a deep nature. They worshipped the earth—*Thorth* or *Teuth*—from whom they themselves claimed to be descended. The thought of the people was forming its deep words long before they came out into speech. Their whole mythology, that dark vast solitude, the home of darkness, the home of light, the great hall of Odin, and other such, belong to a people having deep thoughts lying in it.

The story of the Berserker, which has attracted the attention of antiquaries during the last fifty years, is the personification of what lay deep in the German mind, the wild mind of Germany. The Berserker was one who despised danger and fear, rushed forth fiercely to battle, and, though without armour, trod down hosts of foes like shells under his feet. Hence his name, Berserker, 'bare spirit.' This character is analogous to much that we find in the Germans. Not, certainly, a true sample of their feeling is that constant state of explosive fury which marks the Berserker; yet it illustrates their fundamental character, the strange fierceness called afterwards by Italians the '*furore Tedesco*,' the most dreadful of any. Yet rage of that sort, defying all dangers and obstacles, if kept down sufficiently, is as a central fire, which will make all things to grow on the surface above it. Fighting is the only way it displays itself in the Berserker, but in the Germans at large it appears in many other ways. Well if it never come out in that Berserker Wuth, as it is called. On the whole, it is the best character that can belong to any nation, producing strength of all sorts, and all the concomitants of strength, perseverance, steadiness. It is not easily excited, but when called up, it will have its object accomplished. We find it in all their history.

Justice: that is another of its concomitants. Strength, one may say, is justice itself. The strong man is he that can be just; that sets everything in its own rightful place, one above the other. It is the only way to do anything great and strong; and it is always the boast, and a legitimate one, of this people that they are a just people, framing all their institutions for ends of justice.

Trial by jury is essentially German. Tacitus mentions the existence of an institution precisely analogous to it; and to this day, in one part of Switzerland, there is an old usage of very remote tradition, called the 'street court,' itself quite a rude jury, by which tradition, if two men meet upon the high road, men travelling on business—say carriers, drovers—and one of them do some injury to the other, and they cannot agree about it, they are bound to wait there till seven other persons shall have come up, and these shall judge of the dispute (hence the name 'street court,' 'road court,' 'strasse gericht'); and they are to decide it irrevocably. I say that all the rudiments of our trial by jury exist there in that canton of Switzerland. These few details sufficiently indicate to us what the German character is, and I shall leave you to expand what I have said in your own minds over other traits quite as characteristic.

Before the Reformation even, the Germans had already appeared more than once in modern history. First, when Europe itself was completely destroyed by them; when, after more than two centuries of confused fighting, they at last made peace amongst themselves and joined against Rome, till Europe was altogether abolished, and made anew. This first period, however, was little but a confused delineation of all the influences of that time at work in Europe till the time of Charlemagne. He was also a German, and got all Germany united under him. The modern system of division into kingdoms and principalities came from him.

Their next appearance in the world's history was at the end of the thirteenth and beginning of the fourteenth centuries in Switzerland, for the Swiss are, in fact, Germans. This was the age of Dante. They were the first in modern Europe who attempted to establish a regular government of liberty or freedom. The history of William Tell, a beautiful mythos, is grounded on indisputable facts. Most probably the story of the apple is not true; indeed, it is altogether improbable, as it has been told of others besides Tell; nor that of Gessler's hat either, according to Johannes von Müller. But, what is certain, is that after enduring with extreme patience their wrongs for some space of time, they did contrive to hurl out the Austrian dominion, and to establish in its place a regular government.

This is a thing which reflects great credit on the whole nation of Germans, and leads men to admire them more and more as they consider it. One does not know any instance where the people, during a contest so long and obstinate, have comported themselves so well throughout; enduring their grievances at first, and even sluggishly patient under them; but, finally, these remaining unredressed, rising into a lion-like rage with all the spirit of the Berserker against their tyrants.

Charles the Bold, Duke of Burgundy, was the last to feel their brave resolution. He wanted a kingdom, and for this sole reason contrived to quarrel with them, as he imagined it was quite easy, with his knights and men-at-arms, to overcome these peasants, who fought on foot. He, therefore, made a quarrel with them, but was altogether defeated in three great battles, Granson, Morat, and Nancy, at which last place he wrecked himself against the Swiss. In the first battle, we are told, they knelt down when they saw Charles' immense army coming, as it were, to swallow them up, and prayed that God would that day assist them to fight against their enemies. Comines says that Charles, seeing this, cried: 'See! they yield.' But others, who knew them better, observed that 'they did not much like that species of yielding altogether.' And accordingly they soon found out that there was not much in it to like at all. The Swiss rose like a whirlwind on their enemies, overwhelmed them, and maintained their own rights!

But the third remarkable appearance of the Germans was at the Reformation, and greater than all. This was in the sixteenth century. I have repeatedly alluded to the necessity of change in matters of doctrine, the impossibility of any creed being perpetual, any theory which man's small mind may form of this great universe being complete, though he should study to all eternity the immensity of which he is a fraction. Any opinion he may form will only serve him for a time, it expands itself daily, for progression is the law of every man: if he be a fool even, still, he must have some power of progress; it is inevitable, and his creed will consequently go on expanding by degrees till it gets to its extreme limits, or, if not, till he discovers some ideas which are inconsistent with it, and will produce uneasiness in the mind, to go on increasing generation after generation till it comes at last to spoken protest. Another cause of the ruin of a creed consists in the fact that when the mind begins to be dubious it will rush with double rapidity towards destruction, for all serious men hate dubiety; these view the creed indeed, but if not satisfied with it have done with it for ever. They may decline meddling with it for a long time, but when they come to question it they will have nothing to do with it, they do not want to have popes or priests under any such system. But there is always a number of inferior men who aim at the rewards which the Church has to bestow, and therefore they willingly adhere to it, and the very circumstance of any such attaching themselves to any given system is of itself a certain and infallible cause of ruin to it. This last circumstance was precisely the case with the Roman Catholic Church at this time. There was no Pope Hildebrand then ready to sacrifice life itself to the end that he might make the Church the highest thing in the world.

Any one who was inclined to see things in their proper light then would have decided that it was better to have nothing to do with it, but crouch down in an obscure corner somewhere and read his Bible, and get what good he can for himself in that way, but have nothing to do with the Machiavellian policy of such a Church. The popes of that age were such men as Julius II., Borgia, and Leo X., who did indeed maintain the Church, but as to faith in it, they just believed nothing at all, or believed only that they got so many thousand crowns a year by it; the whole was one chimera, one miserable sham. That change, however, had been working more and more since Dante's time. Dante himself has abundant complaints to make about popes, putting several of them into hell and frightful punishments there, and even earlier than Dante in all literary men we see a more and more growing censoriousness of priests and popes, till in the sixteenth century it had become the fixed idea of all intelligent men, followers of manful and honourable views, that priests and monks were an indolent, useless race who only set themselves against what conduced to human improvement in all departments.

In these circumstances Martin Luther was born. His parents were of the poorest people. His father was a poor miner of Mœrha or Moer, near Eisenach, in Upper Saxony, where Luther was born on November 10th, 1483. He was a man of the largest intellect and learning born in that century, put down by nature as it seemed for the lowest sphere of life, to beat out a little lead ore in his capacity of miner, but it was not so appointed. His father, who seems to have been a remarkable man, contrived to send him to a school, where he struggled on in his studies for a long time. It appears that he went with other of the boys, as was their custom, through the various villages in the intervals of study, singing ballads, and getting in this way a few coppers thrown to him, till at last the widow of a rich burgher, hearing of his ability, assisted him forward, and got him placed at the University, where he soon distinguished himself. His father wished him to be a lawyer, and he was at first studying for that, but afterwards, upon seeing a companion struck suddenly dead by his father's side, Luther, naturally a serious, melancholy-minded man, was so struck to the heart at seeing before his eyes a dear friend at once hurried away into Eternity and infinitude, that the law and the promotions it offered him sank into a poor, miserable dream in comparison to the great reality before him, and he became a monk that he might occupy himself wholly with prayer and religion. He became, as he tells us, 'a strict and painful monk,' and this life continued many years, nearly ten years. He was very miserable in that life, imagining himself doomed to everlasting perdition, and he could not see how prayer, saying of masses, could save him or get him to Heaven. At last one of his brother monks, a pious, good man, told him, what was quite new to him at that time, that the real secret of the thing lay in repentence and faith in Jesus Christ. This was the first insight he ever got into it, that it was not prayer nor masses at all that could save him, but falling down in spirit as Scripture says at the foot of the Cross! At this time, too, he found a Bible, an old Vulgate Bible, in the convent library, which he read, and in this way he got peace of mind at last, but he seems to have introduced no project of reform at the time.

He continued to grow in esteem with everybody. The Elector of Saxony, hearing of his great talents and harmony, brought him to the University he had just founded, and made him one of the professors there. His convent afterwards sent him to Rome, for he still remained an Augustinian monk, to manage some affairs of the convent; this was in the time of Pope Julius II. He was deeply shocked at all he saw there, but was not in the least aware then of the work he was, in a few years, to do. It is a true saying of Schiller's: 'Genius is ever a secret to itself; the strong man is he that is unconscious of his own strength.' But at last Tetzel, the celebrated Dominican, came into Saxony to sell indulgences. He was sent by Pope Leo X., who wanted money for some purpose, some say to buy jewels for a niece, and he sold them there beside Luther. Luther soon found it out in the confessional, as he heard frequently from those who came to confess, that they had no need of repentance for this or that sin, since they had bought indulgences for them! This set Luther to preach a sermon against the sale of indulgences at all, in which he asserted that the Church has only power to remit the penalties itself imposes on sin, but not to pardon sin, and that no man has any authority to do that. Tetzel responded to this, and at last Luther saw himself obliged to look deeper into the matter, and to publish his ninety-five propositions as to indulgences, denying the foundation of the whole matter altogether, and challenging Tetzel to prove it to him either in reason or Scripture. This occasioned a great ferment in Germany, already in an unsettled state of opinion, and produced several missions from the Pope. Cardinal Cajetan tried to persuade him to retract, but, not succeeding, at last brought him before the Diet of Worms. Luther, on the other hand, was going farther and farther off, as his enemies irritated him, seeking to discover what truth there might be in any of the Church's doctrines; till finally, being excommunicated by the Pope, he publicly burned the excommunication in the presence of his friends, and excited thereby a deep murmur of astonished expectancy among the beholders, but nothing more then, though they could not help feeling that the truth must be with him.

A few did stand by him, however; and finally, in the year 1521, the year after that, he surrendered himself to the Diet of Worms, where the Emperor had resolved to have him tried, although he remembered how Huss had been betrayed before, and his safe conduct violated. It was in the eyes of all a daring, great, fearful enterprise, but not fearful to Luther, whose life was not to sink into a downy sleep, while he heard the great call of a far other life upon him, so he determined to go. This was on the 17th of April, 1521. Charles V., the Emperor, and the six Electors were sitting there, and there was he, a poor man, son of a poor miner, with nothing but God's truth for his support. His friends met him at the gate, and told him not to enter the city, as the danger was great; but he told them deliberately 'that, upon the whole, he would go in, though there were as many devils in Worms as house-tiles.' He accordingly appeared, and went through an examination on matters of religion, which was wound up by the question : ' Would he recant his opinions ? '

The answer was to be given on the morrow; he meditated it all the night. Next morning, as he passed through the streets, the people were all on their housetops, calling on him not to deny the truth, and saying, ' Whoso denieth Me before men, him will I deny before My Father.' And there were other voices of that sort which spoke to his heart, but he passed on without a word. In the Council he spoke in reply for two hours, and was admired by everybody for his modest sincerity. 'As to the retractation, he first wished to have explained to him what was wrong in the opinions.' They told him 'that they had nothing to do with scholastic theology, the question was, Would he recant?' To this he answered 'that his book was divided into two portions, part of it was his own, part was Scripture.

K

In the former it was possible that there was much error, which, if proved, he was not only willing, but eager to retract; but as to the other part, he could not retract it. It was neither safe nor prudent to do anything against Conscience; let me,' he said, 'be convicted of error from the Bible, or let the thing stand as written. Here I take my stand; it is neither safe nor prudent to do anything against Conscience; God be my help. Amen!' This speech will be for ever memorable; it was as brave a speech as was ever uttered by man. It was the beginning of things not fully developed even yet, but kindled then first into a flame, which shall never be extinguished. It was the assertion of the right of consulting one's own conscience, which every new founder of a civilisation must now take along with him, which has entered largely into all the activity men have had since!

From this Council he returned to the Convent of Wartzburg, under protection of the Elector of Saxony, where he translated the Bible; and he had twenty-five years of life after this Council: a life of wild struggle, busy and harassed. There is no other finer proof of his greatness than the way he conducted himself while enjoying the confidence of princes; never was his head affected by it, and no judgment ever proceeded from him that was not that of a worthy and brave man. He kept peace between the parties during his life, and soon after his death the war broke out, and the Smalcaldic League was formed.

At Wartzburg, once famous for the Minnesingers, he first translated the Bible into the vulgar tongue. This was the most notable work since Ulphilas' translation into Gothic, made in the fourth century, and it remains to this day a most admirable version.

Luther's character, on the whole, is one of the most characteristic in Germany, of whatsoever is best in German minds. He is the image of a large, substantial, deep man, that stands upon truth, justice, fairness, that fears nothing, considers the right, and calculates on nothing else; and again, does not do it spasmodically, but adheres to it deliberately and calmly, through good report and bad. Accordingly, we find him a good-humoured, jovial, witty man, greatly beloved by every one, and though his words were half battles, as Jean Paul says, stronger than artillery, yet among his friends he was one of the kindest of men. The wild kind of force that was in him appears in the physiognomy of the portrait by Luke Chranak, his painter and friend, the rough plebeian countenance, with all sorts of noble thoughts shining out through it. That was precisely Luther as he appears through his whole history.

Another great German personage, very different from Luther, but who also deserves to be noticed, is Erasmus, a Dutchman (for, as we observed, the Dutch are in fact the same as the Germans, and Erasmus, at any rate, wrote German and spoke it too). His business with respect to the Reformation was trifling, compared to that of Luther. He was sixteen years older than Luther; born at Rotterdam. He, too, like every clear-headed man, was disgusted with that dark ignorance of the monks, and satirised them, and at first admitted the necessity of some kind of reformation, but that he should risk his ease and comfort for it did not enter into his calculations at all; and though he supported Luther at first, he afterwards quarrelled with him, and opposed all his views. He was a great scholar. There was something interesting about his mother's history. His real name had been Gerhardt, but he took that of Erasmus—'love child.' His mother's was a most tragical life; she had been separated from his father by her friends, and he, believing the rumour of her death, made himself a priest; on hearing of which, she sank into an untimely grave.

His mother took him to school. Poor, forlorn woman! she did not know then that he was to become a light of the world! Rudolf Agricola came to the school, and first observing his abilities, took him by the hand and said, 'Study, my little boy; thou shalt be the talk of all men before long.' He subsequently came under the notice of the Archbishop of Paris, who brought him over to England. Afterwards he came frequently to England; he knew More, the Chancellor, intimately. He led from this time a kind of wandering life. Mountjoy, our English Ambassador at Paris, was the first to obtain him a pension. He published many books, among others an edition of the Greek Testament, but the work he was then best known by was the *Praise of Folly*, written here in More's house; it disappoints any one who would read it now. Also he wrote his *Colloquies*, a very ingenious book, and of a great delicacy; indeed, I should say, to make my friends understand the character of Erasmus, that he is more like Addison than any writer I could mention who is familiarly known in this country. I have said what his course was towards the Reformation—that at first he approved of Luther, and then disapproved of him. He was a man certainly of great merit, nor have I much to say against him; yet when I hear historians contrasting him favourably with Luther, and actually upbraiding Luther with him, I must dissent altogether from that, and say that Erasmus is not to be named by the side of Luther; a mere writer of poems, a 'litterateur.' There are many things in Erasmus to object to. Franz Horn is very angry, too, about this setting up of Erasmus, concerning which, I for one, desire nothing more than not to get angry too, and spasmodic, as Luther himself did, in fact, succeed in doing. Franz says Erasmus belonged to a class of people who are very desirous to stand well with God, yet, at the same time, are very loth to stand ill with the devil; who will build a church to God, and a chapel by the side of it for the devil, a sort of position that really is not good in the world.

There is a third striking German character whom

we must notice, **Ulrich** von Hutten. He was a nobleman by birth, destined at first by his father, a rather foolish, obstinate man, to be a monk, which **not wishing to be,** he was then marked **out for a lawyer,** but not that either would he be; till at **last** he got sent by some cousins, who understood **him** better than his father did, to a school or university of some kind, where he occupied himself with literary pursuits. He wrote many books, both in Latin and German, principally in Latin, and became distinguished and known in his own country; but his life was never easy to him. He was a **wanderer all** his days, travelling about to Frankfort and other places, and even to Rome. He was much too headlong a **man; he so** hated injustice that he did **not** know how to deal with **it, and** he became **heartbroken by** it at last.

He had begun before Luther **to** satirise monkery in his 'Epistolæ Obscurorum,' not entirely written by him, indeed; three **or** four of the best heads joined with him in **it. It** is very amusing, but full of all kinds **of** platitudes; a collection of letters supposed to be written by monks, one **monk** writing to another what he intends **to** do, and laying bare all the details of that miserable imbecile life. Erasmus, it is related, burst out laughing on reading it, and by this means broke a suppuration in the throat, which had formed and endangered his life, a thing, therefore, of immense consequence to him. Ulrich had many struggles to meet. His cousin was basely hanged by the Duke of Wirtemberg, assassinated in a wood for some dark purpose. Hutten indignantly pleaded everywhere against the Duke for this, and even went to war with him, in alliance with the free towns then in arms against him. He found it difficult to get any man in office to patronise him. He says of himself that he 'hated tumult' of all kinds; and it was thus a painful and sad position for him—who wished to obey order, while a still higher order commanded him to disobey; when the standing by the existing order would be, in fact, the standing by disorder.

Ulrich was miserably disordered all his life, and wholly without guidance. He, a proud nobleman's son, looked down at first on Luther, a poor monk; but immediately after the Diet of Worms he recognised that Luther was a great man, and soon maintained a correspondence with him. He once wrote to Luther: 'Thy work is of God, and will continue; mine' (his was to force Germany from monkery and oppression), 'mine is of man, and will not continue.' He was much courted and flattered by the Emperor of Germany and other Catholic princes, and even by Francis, the King of the French; but he positively refused to quit Luther's party. A price was set on his head; not exactly that either, but the magistrates of his city had certainly orders to have him sent bound hand and foot to Rome, and murderous assassins were hired to slay him, from all which he was obliged to escape by flight. In that journey he met Hochstratten, the head monk, whom he had **satirised in his** '**Epistolæ** Obscurorum,' and who had ever since raised the prince's ire. **Full of rage,** he dashed down on him, drawing his sword; **but** when the imbecile being who had done him all this mischief uttered a prayer, changing his purpose he hurled him away, and passed on. In this journey, too, he met with Franz von Sickingen, **an** extraordinary, interesting character, and introduced by Goethe into his 'Berlichingen.' Franz gave him shelter in his castle, and here the two first read **Luther's** books, and confessed that the thing **which he** meant, all good men should mean! Ulrich published books, too, in this place.

The **death of** Sickingen contains a very noble thing. He had a feud with the Archbishop **of Trèves, and he** defended himself in his castle on the Rhine, Landstein, **where** the archbishop besieged him; but he could not **be** overcome at all, till one day, while looking at the state of the defences, he was struck by a musket-ball, and died in twenty-four hours after. The castle at once surrendered, as in him the soul of the defence was taken away. And here comes the noble thing I alluded to. At the **point of death,** while he **was** already pale with death, **the archbishop** came **in to see** him, the archbishop who **had** caused his destruction, and Sickingen at once raised his cap, unmindful of the feud, for his reverence for what was above him was far deeper than that; and this seems to me the noblest, politest thing that is recorded of any such moment as that.

Sickingen being killed, Hutten had no resource but again to wander forth; and then occurred the worst thing that I have read of Erasmus, who once, when poor and dependent, flattered Hutten, and obtained his patronage, but was now living at Basle, a rich man, and admitted to the councils of the Emperor. To him Hutten came for relief, but he would have nothing to do with him. Hutten then wrote to his friends, complaining of this miserable treatment of Erasmus, and Erasmus then gave a false account of it in a work he published, whereupon Hutten wrote at last to Erasmus, most indignantly exposing the true affair as a miserably shabby thing to have been perpetrated against a poor man, without hope, without money, without friends! Erasmus then took a violent antipathy to Hutten, and wrote satires upon him; but it was a poor thing that, and he could not clear himself. Hutten then wandered on; but the hand of death was on him. He came to Zurich; but Erasmus wrote beforehand to the magistrates, warning them against him as a hot-headed person, and they forced him to quit the place. He left it, and came to a small island in the lake of Zurich, and died there shortly afterwards. He had maintained a sister up to his death, and at his death there was found in his pocket only one thaler. He died in his thirty-fifth year—one of the bravest men Germany ever had, but of a spirit that could not get to exhibit itself in literature at all; the rough draft of something excellent, but which could not get out into its full delineation.

This must suffice for what can be said of the Reformation in Germany. In my next lecture I shall resume the subject with reference to a country still more interesting to us—namely, our own country.

LECTURE VIII.

May 25th.

SECOND PERIOD—*continued.*

THE ENGLISH: THEIR ORIGIN, THEIR WORK AND DESTINY — ELIZABETHAN ERA — SHAKESPEARE — JOHN KNOX — MILTON — BEGINNING OF SCEPTICISM.

IN our last lecture we introduced ourselves to the German people, the great Teutonic race, and to the great work which was intrusted to them to do by the economy of Providence in this world of ours. We have now to occupy ourselves with one particular tribe of the Teutonic race: whether or not the most important—although from the great things they have had to do we might call it so —it is indisputably the most interesting to us, for it is our own nation, the Saxon or English. This nation, too, first came into decisive notice about the time of the Reformation, and as a nation much connected with that great event. We shall cast a glance over the period which preceded its arriving at the condition of an articulately-speaking nation, when it began partly to understand its own meaning, partly to announce it.

The Saxons are not noticed in the earliest periods by the Romans. They are not even mentioned in Tacitus. In Ptolemy there is but one single line about them. He speaks of 'the Saxons, a people inhabiting the northern part of the Cimbric Chersonesus,' the modern Denmark. But they had come into extraordinary notice from their formidable character in the fourth century, and were, along with the Lombards, the chief fighters of the German tribes. As to their piracies, they were addicted early to the sea; the adventurous of the tribe occupied themselves very much with piracy and sailing of all kinds. Their feats in sailing and fighting excited the greatest terror among the Romans. Sidonius Apollinaris and Ammianus Marcellinus both commemorate the ungovernable temper and wild spirit of this people. Their craft were of a rude description, made of wicker and covered with leather. Gibbon describes their habit of ascending the Rhine in these wicker boats, then carrying them on their shoulders across the country to the Rhone and launching them there, to make their appearance in a short time at the Straits of Gibraltar. Ammianus Marcellinus speaks much of their fondness for the sea. It is curious to see in this manner the ancestors of our Blakes and Nelsons among these people. In general, indeed, a seafaring people is required to be one of the strongest of peoples. Nothing can be a better measure of the strength of a man than to put him into a ship in the middle of the wild elements exposed to the rage and variableness of the winds, which he must observe with an ever-watchful care and shape himself by them, and wait for and seize every favourable instant for the purpose of his enterprise. Accordingly we find that the Dutch and English tribes are the greatest of the Germans. So in Luden or Mascou, I think Mascou, we find the mythus of the creation of the Teutonic people, how one tribe was made out of the mould of the valley of the Danube, another out of water, but the *Saxons* out of the Saxa or rock of the Hartz Mountains. They were, in fact, the hardest of the tribes, and greatly distinguished in that respect from the rest of the Germans; there was a kind of silent ruggedness of Nature in them, with the wild Berserker rage deeper down in the Saxons than in others. They have a kind of resemblance to the Romans in that respect, though much of it has not unfolded itself even among the English, for we have as yet produced no great painter, nor any one who has excelled in the highest arts except Shakespeare, and yet a nation which has produced a Shakespeare we may justly conclude to be capable of producing much. Their talent, however, was practical like that of the Romans, a greatness of perseverance, adherence to a purpose, method—practical greatness in short.

If any seer among them in the year 449, when they landed here in the Isle of Thanet, could have looked forward to the year 1838 as we can look back to 449, he would have said, as we may say, that great and remarkable as the foundation of Rome certainly was, it was not a greater fact, nor so great even, as that humble settlement of the Saxons on these shores. He would have seen our present dominion extending from the Gulf of California, from the mouth of the Gulf of Mexico, away up to the Ganges and Burrampootra, and descending even to our antipodes. He would have seen these descendants of Saxons conquering more than the Romans did, who subdued men, but these subdued the incoherences and difficulties of Nature, reclaiming wild and boundless wastes and converting them into arable land and scenes of civilisation!

For about a hundred years after their landing Saxons continued arriving: one regrets greatly that there is no intelligence to be had about this matter, so full of moment, rude energy, and significance. For three hundred years the war with the Britons, ancient possessors of the soil, lasted; these and the Caledonians were gradually driven back into the mountains, and the Lowlands were made into a Saxon country. To this day 'Saxon' is the Celtic name for the English; the Highland Scotch apply it to the Lowlanders yet. The name 'English' or 'Angles' arose out of a small territory from which they originally came, in the Duchy of Schleswick, where to this day it is called 'Angleland.'

The etymology of the name 'Saxons' is uncertain, nor is it of any value. The opinion seems to be that it is derived from Saks, a sword or knife worn by this people. Nennius has preserved the word of command used by their leader Hengist, '*Niemet hyr Saxas!*' (take your knives). 'Saks' is the Westphalian name yet, or was when Mascou wrote. After these 300 years there remained yet 300 years more of incessant fighting between the different kingdoms of the Heptarchy. We read of battles and successions of kings, and one endeavours to remember them, but without success, except so much of this flocking or fighting as Milton gives us, viz., that they were the battles of kites and crows, for they have no interest for us. Indeed, those who took part in this flocking and fighting were making the reverse of a history of England. Whoever was uprooting a thistle or bramble, or draining out a bog, or building himself a house, or, in short, leaving a single section of order where he had found disorder, that man was writing the history of England, the others were only obstructing it. Yet these battles were natural enough. The people who should succeed in keeping themselves at the top of affairs were the fittest to be there, the weakest would maintain themselves for a while, but when the attack came they would be obliged in every case to surrender to the more force and method that was in the others, which must triumph over all the incoherent characters that needed to be regulated by it. A wild kind of intellect as well as courage was shown by each party in his own department, in his own circumstances.

Traces of deep feeling are scattered over this history, as, indeed, over that of all the Germans. For example, there is the speech of Clotaire, the French king, himself a German, and a remarkable one it is. When he was dying, when he felt himself dying, he exclaimed: 'Wa! Wa! What great God is this that pulls down the strength of the strongest kings?' It was the expression of a wild astonishment in the barbarous mind at the terrible approach of some great unknown thing which he could not escape. There was, too, an affectionateness, a largeness of soul in the intervals of these fights of kites and crows. We often see a prince doing all the good he could, arranging everything as far as it was possible to arrange it.

There was one memorable instance of this— namely, Alfred. He was not exactly the first that united the different kingdoms together, yet we may, on the whole, say that he was the first. He possessed a very great mind, the highest qualification for his office. He lived in a rude, dark age. We all know his fighting against the Danish pirates; his succeeding, after great exertions and fightings, to get his crown back to him again; and how he pacified the country by treaty and wise policy as much as by war. Then in literature his services were, for the age, great; he translated many books from the Latin language into Saxon. He first shaped the thing we call the British Constitution; he laid the foundations of it, as it were. One fancies, too, that he was able to have an instinct into the business, and in that view to lay out institutions which have already lasted 1100 years. He founded Oxford according to tradition, not by the name of university, but at any rate he founded schools there. He was as great a man for this island as Charlemagne was the century before for Europe. His influence was not for the moment felt, but it has borne abundant fruit in after times. Voltaire said of him that he was the greatest man in history—for his self-denial and heroic endeavours on the one hand, and his mild gentleness combined with that on the other.

In the next century, or a century and a half afterwards, the Normans gained possession of the throne of England, an important event, which brought this country into more immediate connexion with the Continent, and produced other results not *all* beneficial in their way. They were the same people (I say this in contradiction to a vague notion which has circulated that, by the Conquest, England became divided into two peoples), who had left their country three or four centuries after the Saxon pirates had come to these shores, and in the course of their emigration had learned a new language by their introduction to the Latin and the French, and had generally attained to a higher culture than the Saxons. They endeavoured, too, to introduce the French language in this country, but wholly failed.

The history of the succeeding periods is but a strange description of elements. There seems to have been nothing but war. At any rate, war was far more frequent here than in any other country; and this lasted down to the very neighbourhood of Queen Elizabeth, for it was not till the reign of her grandfather that the kingdom became consolidated. Nay, Scotland was still more remarkable in this respect. It had been continually fluctuating for six centuries before the end of the Heptarchy, now embracing Cumberland, now confined to the Grampians. But in England, after the Wars of the Roses had been ended, things began to change, till at last the whole amalgamated into some distinct vital unity.

This was begun about the time of Queen Elizabeth, in many respects the summation of innumerable influences, the co-ordination of many things, which till then had been in contest; the first beautiful outflush of energy, the first articulate spoken energy. There was Saxon energy before that, in Hengist and in Horsa; not a spoken energy, but a silent one; not shown in speech, but in work. It was here, as in general, the end of an epoch when it began to speak. The old principle, feudalism, and that other one, the Catholic religion, were beginning to end; when, like the cactus tree, which blooms but once in centuries, so here appeared the blossom of poetry for once, which done, that energy was to carry itself on according to such laws as are suitable to it, abiding till the time of a future manifestation. Nowhere has such a number of great people been at once produced as here in the Elizabethan era—Bacon, Raleigh, Spenser; above all, Shakespeare! It is not possible for us to go through all those names in our short space, and we must therefore confine our attention to Shakespeare alone.

Shakespeare is the epitome of the era of Elizabeth. A man, in whom that era as well as other eras, have found a voice; one who gives utterance to many things silent before him, and worthy to be called the spokesman of our nation! It is now universally admitted that he must be regarded as the greatest person that has been produced in the literature of modern Europe. The Germans have long been as enthusiastic admirers of him as ourselves, and often more enlightened and judicious ones, for there the highest minds have occupied themselves with criticism of Shakespeare. One of the finest things of the kind ever produced is Goethe's criticism on Hamlet in his 'Wilhelm Meister,' which many among you are aware of. I may call it the reproduction of Hamlet in a shape addressed to the intellect, as Hamlet is already addressed to the imagination. Even the French, in late times, have come over to think in the same way. He was one of the great sons of Nature, like a Homer, an Æschylus, a Dante— a voice from the innermost heart of Nature.— He speaks the dialect of the sixteenth century in words much more expressive and comprehensive than any used before him, for knowledge had made great progress in his time, and therefore his language became more complex and rich in significance.

Any one who takes in his likeness accurately must pronounce him *an universal man!* There is no tone of feeling that is not capable of yielding melodious resonance to that of Shakespeare. We have the southern sunny language of his Juliet, the wild northern melody of his Hamlet, varied with most piercing feeling and tones of tenderness; the rude heartfelt humour of his Autolycuses and Dogberrys, and, finally, the great stern Berserker rage burning deep down under all, and making all to grow out in the most flourishing way, doing ample justice to all feelings, not developing any one in particular, but yielding to us all that can be required of him upon every subject. In a word, if I were bound to describe him, I should be inclined to say that his intellect was far greater than that of any other man who has given an account of himself by writing books. I know that there have been distinctions drawn between intellect, imagination, fancy, and so on, and doubtless there are conveniences in such division, but at the same time we must keep this fact in view, that the mind is *one*, and consists not of bundles of faculties at all, showing ever the same features however it exhibits itself—whether in painting, singing, fighting, ever with the same physiognomy. And when I hear of the distinction between the poet and the thinker I really see no difference at all, for the poet is really such by dint of superior vision, by dint of a more deep serene vision, and he is a poet solely in virtue of that. Thus I can well understand how the Duke of Marlborough once declared that all his acquaintance with the history of England was owing to Shakespeare. One can understand it, I say, for Shakespeare arrived at more of the meaning of history than many books written on history could have done. His intellect seized at once what was the proper object of historical interest, and put it down there as the leading incident of his play. The trace of intellect is more legible in Shakespeare than in any other writer. Bacon, indeed, was great, but not to be compared with Shakespeare. He not only *sees* the object but *sees through it*, sympathises with it, and makes it his own. Let us look into the scheme of his works, the play of Hamlet, for instance. Goethe found out, and has really made plausible to his readers, all sorts of harmonies in the structure of his plays with the nature of things, and we have realised in this way all that could be demanded of him. And what is still more excellent, I am sure that Shakespeare himself had no conception at all of any such meaning in his poem; he had no scheme of the kind. He would just look into the story, his noble mind, the serene depth of it, would look in on it as it was by nature, with a sort of noble instinct, and in no other way. If he had written a criticism upon it he would not at all have said what Goethe said about it. And thus when we hear of so much said of the art of any great writer it is not *art* at all, it is properly *nature*.

It is not known to the author himself, but is the instinctive behest of his mind. This all-producing earth knows not the symmetry of the oak which springs from it. It is all beautiful, not a branch is out of its place, all is symmetry there; but the earth has itself no conception of it, and produced it solely by the virtue that was in itself. So is the case with Homer; and then critics slip in in the rear of these men and mark down the practice they followed, and prescribe it to others for imitation, forgetting that the very thing to be prescribed is the healthy mind of these men, which of itself knows what to put down and what to omit in the beautiful sympathy of brotherhood with their subject, but not how to follow certain prescribed rules about beginning in the middle, end, or beginning of the subject, and other rules of that sort.

I have generally found that morals in a man are the counterpart of the intellect that is in him. In fact, morality is the noblest force in his mind, the soul of his soul, and must lie at the root of all the great things he could utter. In Shakespeare, then, there are always the noblest sympathies, no sectarianism, no cruelty, no narrowness, no vain egotism; he is the best illustration we could have of what I am always talking about, consciousness and unconsciousness. The things great and deep in him he seems to have no notion of at all. Occasionally we have certain magniloquent passages which at this day we can scarcely understand, often bombastic, vastly inferior to his ordinary compositions, and these he seems to have imagined extraordinarily great; but, in general, there is a fervent sincerity in any matter he undertakes, by which one sees at once as through a window into the beautiful greatness of the soul of man. And as to his life, what a beautiful life was that, amid trials enough to break the heart of any other man. Poverty, and a mean poor destiny, which if he were an ambitious man would have driven him mad, but he would not suffer himself to be subdued by it. And it was fortunate for us. If he had been suffered to live quietly in Warwickshire his mind was so rich in itself he would have found such 'sermons in stones and good in everything' that he would probably not have troubled the world at all with his productions. It is thus that in all departments of thought an accidental thing, the action of accident, becomes often of the greatest importance. For the greatest man is always a quiet man by nature, we are sure not to find greatness in a prurient noisy man. Thus Shakespeare at first lived, running about the woods in his youth, together with, as we find by dim traditions, all the wild frolic of that age and place. Stealing deer and the like feats of ebullient buoyancy, till distress sends him to London to write his immortal plays there! And I will here, before concluding my remarks on Shakespeare, add a few words on the conditions under which all human things are to be written. We must say that what the critics talk about, the harmony of the poet's purpose is not true. In

Shakespeare's plays **genius** is under fetters, he has in general taken **some old** story and used that for the subject of his play, with the mere purpose to gather an audience to the Bankside Theatre; this was the only problem he had to resolve, Nature and his own noble mind did the rest. In consequence of this we find in some of his pieces many things vague and quite unsatisfactory, and are unable to discover any significance about them, but ever and anon we see a burst of truth, and are forced to exclaim, 'Yes, that is true!' That is the case with the delineation of human feelings in every age.

I shall now very reluctantly leave Shakespeare, and direct your notice to another great man, very different from Shakespeare—John Knox. He and Shakespeare lived in the same age; he was, indeed, sixty years old when Shakespeare was born, but, at any rate, both lived in the same age together. Of him it may be said, that if Shakespeare was the most giant-like man, and the highest of poets, John Knox seems, if one knew him rightly, to have been as entirely destitute of immorality as Shakespeare was of prose.

I cannot, however, think that he is to be compared with Luther, as some of the Germans in these days have done, who have set him even above Luther; struck with the great veracity of Knox. Luther would have been a great man in other things besides the Reformation; a great, substantial, happy man, who must have excelled in whatever matter he undertook. Knox had not that faculty, but simply this, of standing entirely upon truth; it is not that his sincerity is known to him to be sincerity, but it arises from a sense of the impossibility of any other procedure. He has been greatly abused by many persons for his extremely rough and uncourteous behaviour, for he had a terrible piece of work to do. He has been even represented as struggling for a mere whim of his own, regardless altogether of other things. But that charge is not true, and as to that moral rigour of his, it is the great thing after all: *given* a sincere man, you have *given* a thing worth attending to. Since sincerity, what is it but a divorce from earth and earthly feelings. The sun, which shines upon the earth, and seems to touch it, does not touch the earth at all. So the man who is free of earth is the only one that can maintain the great truths of existence, not by an ill-natured talking for ever about truth, but it is he who does the truth. And this is a great and notable object to be attended to, for that is the very character of Knox. He was called out to free a people from dark superstitions and degradations into life and order. It is very notable that at first he had no idea of being a reformer, although he had a clear sound view that Protestantism must be the true religion, and the Catholic religion false. Though a monk, he determined now to have nothing to do with Catholicism, and he withdrew from all prominence in the world until he had reached the age of forty-three, an age of quietude and composure. When he was besieged in the Castle of St. Andrew's along with his master, whose children he educated, he had many conferences with his master's chaplain. The latter, having first consulted with the people, **who were anxious** to **hear** Knox preach too, suddenly addressed **him** from the pulpit, saying that 'it was not right for him to sit still when great things were to be spoken; that the harvest was great, but the labourers were few; that he (the chaplain) was not so great a man as Knox, and that all were desirous to hear the latter; is it not so, brethren?' he asked, to which they assented. Knox then had to get into the pulpit, trembling, with a pale face, and finally he burst into tears, and came down, not having been able to say a word.

From this time he wandered about, resisting the **destiny** that was for him, until at last he dared not refuse any more. It was a fiery kind of baptism **that** initiated him. He **had become a preacher** not **three** months, when the castle surrendered, and they were all taken prisoners and worked **as** galley slaves on the river Loire, confined for life there. The chiefs of the conspirators were put in prison; this was the year forty-seven or forty-nine, from which his whole life forward was as a battle. Seven years after we find him escaping from the French galleys, **when** he came to England.

In Luther **we** often see an overshadowing **of** despair, and especially towards the end of his life, **when he describes** himself as 'heartily sick of existence, and most desirous that his Master would call **him to** his rest.' Another time he laments the hopelessness of Protestantism, and says that all sects will rise up at last in the day of judgment. But there never was anything like this in Knox; he never gave up, even in the water of the Loire. They were ordered to hear mass; but though they went to hear it, they could not be prevented from putting on their caps during it. Their Virgin Mary was once brought for some kind of reverence to the people in the galley, and it was handed to Knox first; but he saw nothing there but a painted piece of wood—a 'pented bredd,' as he called it in his Scotch dialect; and on their pressing him, he threw it into the water, saying that 'the Virgin, being wooden, would swim.' There was a great deal of humour in Knox, as bright a humour as in Chaucer, expressed in his own quaint Scotch. He wrote the History of the Scotch Reformation. By far better than any other history is that autobiography of his. Above all, there is in him a genuine natural rusticity, a decided earnestness of purpose; the good nature and humour appear in a very striking way, not as a sneer altogether, but as real delight at seeing ludicrous objects. Thus, when he describes the two archbishops quarrelling, no doubt he was delighted to see the disgrace it brought on their church; but he was chiefly excited by the really ludicrous spectacle of rochets flying about and vestments torn, and the struggle each made to overturn the other.

The sum of the objections made to Knox, and which have obfuscated and depressed his memory for centuries, seems to be his intolerance; that he wanted tolerance and all the qualities that follow out of it; and particularly for his rude, brutal way of speaking to Queen Mary. Now, I confess that when I came to read these very speeches, my opinion of these charges was that they are quite undeserved. It was quite impossible for any man to do Knox's functions and be civil too; he had either to be uncivil, or to give up Scotland and Protestantism altogether. Mary wanted to make of Scotland a mere shooting-ground for her uncles, the Guises. In many respects she seems to have been a weak, light-headed woman, and Knox, in the question between civility and duty, was bound to stand by the latter and not by the former; but his incivility was not at all rude or brutal; it was nothing more than the statement of what was necessary to be done. It was unfortunate, too, for him that the sovereign was a woman, that he had not a man to deal with; there would have been less commiseration then, and he would not have been afraid to speak in the same way to a man if one had been there. It was truly said of him on his death-bed by the Earl of Morton: 'There he lies that never feared the face of man!' When I look at what he had to do; at the wild people, the barbarous horde he found it; and how he left it a quiet, civilised one, and how he brought down into the meanest minds, into every hut of Scotland, the greatest thoughts that ever were in the mind of man, I cannot but admire him, and expect all honest people to do the same, however they may differ from him in opinion. We cannot expect all men's opinions to tally with our own. It ought to be enough for us that there is sincerity of belief, of conviction.

The third person to whom I have to direct your attention is Milton. He lived a century from Knox, and he may be considered as a summing up, composed, as it were, of the two—of Shakespeare and Knox. As to Shakespeare, one does not find what religion he was of; an universal believer, impressed with many things which may be called religious; having reverence for everthing that bore the mark of the Deity, but of no particular sect, not particularly Protestant more than Catholic. But Milton was altogether sectarian—a Presbyterian, one might say. He got his knowledge out of Knox, for Knox's influence was not confined to Scotland. It was planted there at first, and continued growing in his own country till it filled it, and then it spread itself into England, working great events, and finally, after causing the quarrel between Scotland and Charles I., it ended in the Revolution of 1688, an event the effects of which benefit England to this day.

Milton learned much of Knox. He was partly the religious philosopher, partly the poet, for it must be a little mind that cannot see that he was a poet—one of the wild Saxon mind, full of deep religious melody that sounds like cathedral music. However, he must not be ranked with Shakespeare.

He stands relative to Shakespeare as Tasso or Ariosto does to Dante, as Virgil to Homer. He is conscious of writing an epic, and of being the great man he is. No great man ever felt so **great** a consciousness as Milton. That consciousness was the measure of his greatness; he was not one of those who reach into actual contact with the deep fountain of greatness. His 'Paradise Lost' is not an epic in its composition as Shakespeare's utterances are epic. It does not come out of the heart of things; he hadn't it lying there to pour it out in one gush; it seems rather to have been welded together afterwards. **His** sympathies with things are much narrower than Shakespeare's—too sectarian. In universality of mind there is no hatred; it doubtless **rejects** what is displeasing, but not in hatred **for it.** Everything has a right to exist. **Shakespeare** was not polemical: Milton **was** polemical altogether.

Milton's disquisitions on these subjects are quite wearisome to us now. 'Paradise Lost' is a very ambitious poem, a great picture painted on huge canvas; but it is not so great a thing as to concentrate our minds upon the deep things within ourselves as Dante does, to show what a beautiful thing the life of man is; it is to travel with paved streets beside us rather than lakes of fire. This Dante has done, and Milton **not.** There is no life in Milton's characters. Adam and Eve are beautiful, graceful objects, but no one has breathed the Pygmalion life into them; they remain cold statues. Milton's sympathies were with things rather than with men, the scenery and phenomena of nature, the trim gardens, the burning lake; but as for the phenomena of the mind, he was not able to see them. He has no delineations of mind except Satan, of which we may say that Satan was his own character, the black side of it. I wish, however, to be understood not to speak at all in disparagement of Milton; far from that.

In our next lecture we shall notice French literature.

LECTURE IX.

THIRD PERIOD.

VOLTAIRE — THE FRENCH — SCEPTICISM — FROM RABELAIS TO ROUSSEAU.

Of this Lecture no record exists.

LECTURE X.

June 1st.

THIRD PERIOD—*(continued).*

EIGHTEENTH CENTURY IN ENGLAND—WHITFIELD—SWIFT—STERNE—JOHNSON—HUME.

In our lecture of this day we shall cast an eye upon England during the eighteenth century, a period of wide consequence to us, and therefore most interesting to us now in the nineteenth century.

In our last lecture we saw the melancholy phenomenon of a system of beliefs which had grown up for 1800 years, and had formed during that period great landmarks of the thought of man, crumbling down at last, and dissolving itself in suicidal ruin; and we saw one of the most remarkable nations of men engaged in destroying: nothing growing in the great seed-field of time, so that well might Goethe say, 'My inheritance, how bare! Time, how bare!' For everything man does is as seed cast into a seed-field, and there it grows on for ever. But the French sowed nothing. Voltaire, on the contrary, casting firebrands among the dry leaves, produced the combustion we shall notice by-and-by. Of Voltaire himself we could make but little—a man of a great vivacity of mind, the greatest acuteness, presenting most brilliant coruscations of genius, but destitute of depth, scattering himself abroad upon all subjects, but in great things doing nothing except to canker and destroy. This being once conceived, that the people had fallen into scepticism, we can imagine that all other provinces of thought were quite sure of being cultivated in the same unfruitful desert manner—politics, for instance. In France, too, appeared Mably, Montesquieu, and an innumerable host of other writers of the same sort, finally summed up in the *Contrat Social* of Rousseau. The only use to which they put the intellect was not to look outwardly upon nature, and love or hate as circumstances required, but to inquire why the thing was there at all, and to account for it and argue about it.

So it was in England too, and in all European countries. The two great features of French intellect were formalism and scepticism. These became the leading intellectual features of all the nations of that century. French literature got itself established in all countries. One of the shallowest things that has ever existed, it never told man anything; there never was any message it had to deliver him. But, on the other hand, it was the most logically precise of all; it stood on established rules, and was the best calculated to make its way among nations.

Even in Germany it became so popular that, for a time, it actually seemed to have extirpated the public mind. In England too, and in Spain, where it was introduced by the Bourbon sovereigns, and where the beautiful literature of Cervantes dwindled away before it, so as never to have recovered itself since. It is not because any particular doctrine is questioned, but because society gets unbelieving altogether, and faith gets dwindled altogether into mere chimeras, so that, to an observer, it might be doubtful whether the whole earth were not hypothetical. He sees the quack established; he sees truth trodden down to the earth everywhere around him; in his own office he sees quackery at work, and that part of it which is done by quackery is done better than all the rest; till at last he, too, concludes in favour of this order of things, and gets himself enrolled among this miserable set, eager after profit, and of no belief except the belief always held among such persons, that *Money will buy money's worth*, and that *Pleasure is pleasant*. But woe to that land and its people if, for what they do, they expect payment at all times! It is bitter to see. Such times are extremely painful— as it were, the winter weather of the state. Woe to the state if there comes no spring! All men will suffer from it with confusion in the very heart of them.

In England this baneful spirit was not so deep as in France, and for several reasons. One was that their nature, the Teutonic nature, is much slower than the **French**; much deeper, not so absorbed at any time as the French has been, whether with scepticism or more worthy things. Another reason was that England was a Protestant, free country, and, as contra-distinguished from France, a well-regulated country. An Englishman, too, will moderate his opinions, and at any time keep them to himself. We find many simply trusting themselves to the examination of the great things of the world, but notwithstanding barely keeping out of this dark region of complete scepticism, and doing many things hearty and manly in spite of that. In France, on the contrary, all things were in an extremely bad state, much depending on Jesuits. In the eighteenth century, however—here with us a century of disputation, if not of complete unbelief—a century of contrariety, there was nothing to be found but argument everywhere.

Never before was there so much argument, literary argument in particular. All things were brought down to the one category of argument; from controversies about Dr. Sacheverell, through the whole range of metaphysics, up to the Divine legation of Moses, essays on miracles, and the like, by men like Hume and Paley, and down to the writers of our own time. Nichols' *Anecdotes of the Eighteenth Century*, an interesting book, offers a curious picture of this state of things. Nine-tenths of his anecdotes are about the Church and Church questions, as if the human intellect had nothing to do but with polemics. Now, though I do all honour to logic in its place, I will venture to say that such subjects as these, high subjects of faith in religion, faith in polity, are as good as lost if there be no other way than by logic to take them up. I must impress upon your minds the words of Goethe: 'The highest is not capable of being spoken *outwards* at all.' Ever has deep secrecy been observed in sacred things. Pompey could not understand this, when he sought to discover what veiled thing that was in the temple of Jerusalem.

Among the Egyptians, too, there was the veiled figure of Saïs, not to be looked upon. And secrecy denotes importance in much lower things than that. A man who has no secrecy in him is still regarded as having no kind of sense in him for apprehending whatever is greatest and best in the world. I admire much that inscription in the Swiss gardens, 'Speech is silvern, silence is golden!' After speech has done its best, silence has to include all that speech has forgotten or cannot express. Speech is of time, of to-day; eternity is silent. All great things are silent. Whenever they get to be debated on by logic, they are as good as lost. It is impossible to prove faith or morality by speech at all, for logic, if we consider it, what does it mean? It pretends to enforce men to adopt a belief, and yet there is no such constraint possible in that way. Looking at the whole circle of things summoned before logic, I do not find more than one single object taken in by logic entirely, and that is Euclid's Elements.

In other respects logic, speaking accurately, can do no more than define to others what it is *you* believe; and when you have so done, a mind made like yours, which sees that you believe, will perhaps believe also. But in mathematics, where things are called by certain simple and authorised designations, there alone is it final, as that two and two make four, the angle in a semicircle is a right angle. But where men are not even agreed on the meaning of the appellations, the case is different, as, for instance, Virtue is utility,—try that. In every different mind there will be a different meaning of the words virtue and utility. Let them state the belief as they can, but not attempt to confine it in the narrow bounds of logic. In spite of early training, I never do see sorites of logic hanging together, put in regular order, but I conclude that it is going to end in some *niaiserie*, in some miserable delusion.

However imperfect the literature of England was at this period, its spirit was never greater. It did great things, it built great towns, Birmingham and Liverpool, Cyclopean workshops, and ships. There was sincerity there at least. Richard Arkwright, for instance, who invented the spinning jennies, he was a sincere man. Not as in France. Watt, too, was evidently sincere in that province of activity. Another singular symptom of the earnestness of the period was that thing we call Methodism. It seems to have merely gathered up a number of barren formulas, with little inspiration in it at first, as it exhibited itself in the rude hearts of the common people. Much of its success was due to Whitfield, who must have been a man with great things in his heart. He had many dark contests with the spirit of denial that lay about him before he called his genius forth into action. All the *logic* in him was poor and trifling compared to the *fire* that was in him, unequalled since Peter the Hermit. First he went to Bristol, and preached to the neighbouring coal miners, who were all heathens yet, but he preached to them till he saw, as he tells us, 'their black cheeks seamed with white tears.' He came to Scotland, and got money there to convert the heathen. This was a great thing to do, considering the hard, thrifty, cold character of the nation. He came to Glasgow and preached, and talked about the Indians and their perishing state; would they hesitate to contribute of their goods to rescue this poor people? And thus he warmed the icy people into a flame, insomuch that, not having money enough by them, they ran home for more, and brought even blankets, farm stuff, hams, &c., to the church, and piled them in a heap there! This was a remarkable fact, whether it were the work of a good spirit, or of the devil. It is wonderful that it did not strike Hume more when he heard Whitfield on the Calton Hill.

When we look at the literature of the times, we see little of that spirit which is to be sought for in the steam engines. We have no time to mention Dryden, a great poet put down in the worst of times, and thus a formalist; a man whose soul was no longer in contact with anything he got to delineate; for ever thinking of the effect he was to produce on the court, and for this end he adopted French plays as the model of his own. He, I say, became a formalist, instead of quietly and silently delineating the thought that was in him. But Dryden must not be censured for it; his poverty was the cause, not his will. He changed to be a Roman Catholic at last. A man of immense intellect: it is displayed in his translation, for example, of the *Æneid*, which contains many beautiful and sounding things.

In Queen Anne's time, after that most disgraceful class of people—King Charles' people—had passed away, there appeared the milder kind of unbelief. Complete formalism is the characteristic of Queen Anne's reign. But, amid all this, it is strange how many beautiful indications there are of better things, how many truths were said. Addison was a mere lay preacher, completely bound up in formalism, but he did get to say many a true thing in his generation; an instance of one formal man doing great things. Steele had infinitely more *naïveté*, but he was only a fellow-soldier of Addison, to whom he subordinated himself more than was necessary. It is a cold vote in Addison's favour that one gives.

By far the greatest man of that time, I think, was Jonathan Swift: Dean Swift, a man entirely deprived of his natural nourishment, but of great robustness; of genuine Saxon mind, not without a feeling of reverence, though, from circumstances, it did not awaken in him, for he got unhappily, at the outset, into the Church, not having any vocation for it. It is curious to see him arranging, as it were, a little religion to himself. Some man found him one day giving prayers to his servants in a kind of secret manner, which he did, it seems, every morning, for he was determined, at any rate, to get out of cant; but he was a kind of cultivated heathen, no Christianity in him. He saw himself in a world of confusion and falsehood. No eyes were clearer to see into it than his. He was great from being of acrid temperament: painfully sharp nerves in body as well as soul, for he was constantly ailing, and his mind, at the same time, was soured with indignation at what he saw around him. He took up therefore, what was fittest for him, namely, sarcasm, and he carried it quite to an epic pitch. There is something great and fearful in his irony, for it is not always used for effect, or designedly to depreciate. There seems often to be a sympathy in it with the thing he satirises; occasionally it was even impossible for him so to laugh at any object without a sympathy with it, a sort of love for it; the same love as Cervantes universally shows for his own objects of merit. In his conduct, there is much that is sad and tragic, highly blameable; but I cannot credit all that is said of his cruel unfeeling dissipation. There are many circumstances to show that by nature he was one of the truest of men, of great pity for his fellow-men. For example, we read that he set up banks for the poor Irish in his neighbourhood, and required nothing of them but that they should keep their word with him, when they came to borrow. 'Take your own time,' he said, 'but don't come back if you fail to keep the time you tell me.' And if they had failed, he would tell them, 'Come no more to me, if you have not so much method as to keep your time; if you cannot keep your word, what are you fit for?' All this proves him to have been a man of much affection, but too impatient of others' infirmities. But none of us can have any idea of the bitter misery which lay in him; given up to ambition, confusion, and discontent. He fell into fatalism at last, and madness, that was the end of it. The death of Swift was one of the awfullest; he knew his madness to be coming. A little before his death he saw a tree withered at the top, and he said that, 'like that tree, he, too, was dying at the top.' He was well called by Johnson a driveller and a show, a stern lesson to ambitious people.

Another man of much the same way of thinking, and very well deserving notice, was Laurence Sterne. In him also there was a great quantity of good struggling through the superficial evil. He terribly failed in the discharge of his duties, still, we must admire in him that sportive kind of geniality and affection, still a son of our common mother, not cased up in buckram formulas as the other writers were, clinging to forms, and not touching realities. And, much as has been said against him, we cannot help feeling his immense love for things around him; so that we may say of him, as of Magdalen, 'much is forgiven him, because he loved much.' A good simple being after all.

I have nothing at all, in these limits, to say of Pope. It is no use to decide the disputed question as to whether he were a poet or not, in the strict sense of the term; in any case, his was one of the finest heads ever known, full of deep sayings, uttered in the shape of couplets—rhymed couplets.

The two persons who exercised the most remarkable influences upon things during the eighteenth century were, unquestionably, Samuel Johnson and David Hume: two summits of a great set of influences, two opposite poles of it—the one a puller down of magnificent, far-reaching thoughts; the other, most excellent, serious, and a great conservative.

Samuel Johnson, in some respects, stood entirely alone in Europe. In those years there was no one in Europe like him. For example, the defenders of what existed in France were men who did nothing but mischief by their falsehoods and insincerity of all kinds.

Johnson was a large-minded man, an entirely sincere and honest man. Whatever may be our differences of opinion is here entirely insignificant; he must inevitably be regarded as the brother of all honest men. One who held this truth among the insincerities that lay around him, that, after all, 'life was true yet,' and he was a man to hold by that truth, and cling to it in the general shipwreck on the sea of Eternity. All would be over with him without it; he knew that, and acted up to it. Hardly has any man ever influenced more an existing state of things. He produced in England that resistance to the French Revolution, commonly called Pittism, by demonstrating its necessity in the most perfect sincerity of heart. A man whose life was, in the highest degree, miserable; hardly any man, not even Swift, suffered so much as Johnson in the first part of his life. He was a 'much enduring man!' A man of a most unhealthy body, for ever sick and ailing. When he was at Oxford, a sizar there, so great was his poverty that he had no shoes to his feet, and used to walk about putting his bare feet into the mud of the streets. A charitable man, seeing this, put a pair of shoes at his door for him, but this irritated Johnson as a reflection on his poverty, and he flung them out of window, rather than use them. Then he fell sick over and over again. Those about him regarded him as a man that had gone mad, and was more fit for Bedlam than anything else.

After he left Oxford, he tried to be a schoolmaster, but, failing in that, came to London to try his fortune there. There he lived on fourpence a day, sometimes having no home, and reduced to sleep on bulks and steps, at other times to stay in cellars. And I must regard him as one of the greatest heroes, since he was able to keep himself erect amid all that distress : he shook it from him as the lion shakes the dewdrops from his mane! He had no notion of becoming a great character at all, he only tried not to be killed with starvation! And though it is mournful to think that a man of the greatest heart should have suffered so much, we must consider that this suffering produced that enterprise in him, and at last he did get something to do; his object was not to go about seeking to know the reasons of things in a world where there is much to be *done*, little to be *known*; for the great thing, above all others, is what a man can *do* in this world!

There is not such a cheering spectacle in the eighteenth century anywhere as Samuel Johnson. He contrived to be devout in it, he had a belief and held by it; a genuine inspired man. And it is a great thing to think that Johnson had one who could appreciate him; any one must love poor Boswell, who (not fixing his eyes on the vain and stupid things in 'Bozzy's' character) remarks that beautiful reverence and attachment he had for Johnson, putting them side by side, this great mass of a plebeian and this other conceited Scotch character: full of the absurd pretensions of my country's gentlemen, noting down and treasuring with reverence the sayings and anecdotes of this great, shaggy, dusty pedagogue. And really, he has made of these things a book, which is a most striking book, and likely to survive long after him; a kind of epic poem, by which **Johnson** must long continue in the first ranks of English biography.

But we must now come to a very different personage, Hume. Hume was born in the same year with Johnson, whom he so little resembles. He, too, is deserving to be looked at. Very nearly of Johnson's magnitude, and quite as sincere, but of a far duller kind of sense. His eye, unlike Johnson's, was not open to faith; yet he was of a noble perseverance, a silent strength, and he showed it in his very complicated life, as it lay before him. He could not go into commerce, for his habits as the son of a gentleman were averse to it. Yet his parents wishing him to make money in some way, he was set to various things, and finally sent to Bristol to be a merchant. But, after trying and struggling with it for two years, he found he could not go on, and he felt a strong thirst to prosecute the cultivation of learning, so that he abandoned the other for that.

He tried to get appointed a professor in the University of Edinburgh, but they would not have him, so he retired to live upon sixty pounds a year in a small town in Brittany, called La Flèche, where he began writing books, and thus got distinguished. He was not at any time patronised by any considerable class of persons, though latterly he was noticed by a certain class. The rich people did look after him at last, but a general recognition in his day he never got. His chief work, the *History of England,* failed to get buyers. He bore it all like a stoic, like a heroic, silent man as he was, and then proceeded calmly to the next thing he had to do. I have heard old people, who have remembered Hume well, speak of his great good humour under trials, the quiet strength of it, the very converse in this of Dr. Johnson, whose coarseness was equally strong with his heroism. Then, as to his methodicalness, no man ever had a larger view than Hume; he always knows where to begin and end. In his history he frequently rises, though a cold man naturally, into a kind of epic height as he proceeds. His description of the Commonwealth, for example, where all is delineated as with a crayon; one sees there his large mind, moreover, not without its harmonies. As to his scepticism, that is perfectly transcendental, working itself out to the very end. He starts with *Locke's Essay*, thinking, as was then generally thought, that logic is the only way to the truth. He began with this, and went on; in the end he exhibited to the world his conclusion, that there was nothing at all credible or demonstrable, the only thing certain to him being that he himself existed and sat there, and that there were some species of things in his own brain. Any other man to him was only a spectrum, not a reality. Now it was right that this should be published, for if that were *all* that lay in scepticism, the making that known was extremely beneficial to us; he did us great service in that; then all would see what was in it, and accordingly would give up the unprofitable employment of spinning cobwebs of logic in their brain—no one would go on spinning them much longer.

Hume, too, is very remarkable as one of the three historians we have produced, for his history, an able work for the time, shows far more insight than either Robertson or Gibbon. Robertson was, in fact, as Johnson thinks him, a shallow man. In his conversation with Boswell about him, we have Johnson always contradicting Robertson; yet there was a power of arrangement in Robertson: no one knew better where to begin a story and where to stop. This was the greatest quality in him, that and a soft sleek style. On the whole, he was merely a politician, open to the common objection to all the three, that total want of belief; and worse in Robertson, a minister of the Gospel, preaching, or pretending to preach. A poor notion of moral motives he must have had; in his description of Knox, for instance, he can divine no better motive for him than a miserable hunger, love of plunder, and the influence of money; and such was Hume's view also! The same is remarkable of Gibbon in a still more contemptible way—a greater historian than Robertson, but not so great as Hume. With all his swagger and bombast, no man ever gave a more futile account of human things than he has done of the decline and fall of the Roman Empire; assigning no profound cause for these phenomena, nothing but diseased nerves, and all sorts of miserable motives, to the actors in them.

So that the world seemed then to present one huge imbroglio of quackery, and men of nobleness could only despise and sneer at it.

On Friday next (not Monday) we shall resume this discussion, and shall remark the downfall and consummation of scepticism; for, thank God, its time was short.

LECTURE XI.

June 8th.

THIRD PERIOD—*(continued)*.

CONSUMMATION OF SCEPTICISM — WERTHERISM — THE FRENCH REVOLUTION.

We traced the history of scepticism in literature in our last lecture down to David Hume, the greatest of all the writers of his time, and in some respects the worthiest. To-day we shall delineate the consummation of scepticism.

It is very strange to look at scepticism in contrast with a thing that preceded it; to contrast, for example, David Hume with Dante, two characters distant by five centuries from one another, two of the greatest minds in their respective departments (the mind of both was to do the best that could be done in their existing circumstances); to contrast them, I say, and see what Dante made of it and what Hume made of it.

Dante saw a solemn law in the universe, pointing out his destiny with an awful and beautiful certainty, and he held to it. Hume could see nothing in the universe but confusion, and he was certain of nothing but his own existence; yet he had instincts which were infinitely more true than the logical part of him, and so he kept himself quiet in the middle of it all, and did no harm to any one; for as to his books, he believed that they were true, and therefore to publish them he was bound—bound to do what seemed right to him. He had no other business for his intellect than this, and, moreover, as I have observed, in publishing them he did a useful service for humanity.

But scepticism, however much called for at that time, particularly in France, cannot be considered other than a disease of the mind; a fatal condition to be in, it seems to me, or at best useful only as a means to get at knowledge. For the thing is, not to find out what is *not true*, but what *is true*. Surely that is the real design of man's intelligence! But as to this overspreading our whole mind with logic, it was altogether a false and unwarranted attempt, considering logic as the only means to attain to truth, and that things did not exist at all except some one stood up and could mark the place that they occupied in the world; forgetting that it is always great things that do not speak at all. If a truth must not be believed except demonstrable by logic, we had better go away without it altogether.

And it was not only the disbelievers in religion that were sceptic at that time; but the whole system of mind was sceptic. The defenders of

Christianity were sceptic, too, for ever trying to prove the **truth** of their doctrines by logical evidences. What is the use of attempting to prove motion? The philosopher was right who got up and began to walk instead. So with religion. It may seem a plausible, but it is a **vain** attempt to demonstrate by logical arguments what must be always unspeakable. But this habit had in the eighteenth century **overrun all** the provinces of thought. Nothing but that was serviceable or useful in the eyes of that generation. An indication of an unhealthy mind, that system of trying to make out a theory on every subject. It is good, doubtless, that there should always be some theory formed, with a view to the apprehension of a subject, but as for any other view it is impossible. For example, there is a kind of theory in what we have been following out—what we call the history of European culture; we use it for facility of arrangement. But there is a wide difference between a theory of this kind and a theory by which we profess to account for it, and give the reasons for its being there at all.

Accordingly, there is only one theory (as I observed at the beginning of these lectures) which has been most triumphant—that of the planets. On no other subject has any other theory succeeded so far; yet even that is not perfect. The astronomer knows one or two planets, we may say; but he does not know *what they are*, where they are going, or whether the solar system is not itself drawn into a larger system of the kind. In short, with every theory the man who knows something about it knows mainly this—that there is much uncertainty in it, great darkness about it, extending down to infinite deeps; in a word, that he does not know what it is. Let him take the stone, for example—the pebble that lies under his feet. He knows that it is a stone, broken out of rocks old as the creation; but what that pebble is he knows not; he knows nothing at all about that.

This system of making a theory about everything was what we can call an enchanted state of mind. That man should be misled; that he should be deprived of knowing the truth, that this world is a reality, and not a huge, confused hypothesis; that he should be deprived of this by the very faculties given him to understand it, I can call by no other name than enchantment. Everything was placed upon the single table of logic; one could hardly go anywhere without meeting some pretentious theory or other. Even the very centre of all was brought to that level—morals. There was a theory of virtue and vice; duty and the contrary of that. This will come to be thought one day an extraordinary sort of procedure. When I think of this, it seems to me more and more that morality is the very centre of the existence of man; that there is nothing for a man but that which it is his duty to do. It is the life, the harmonious existence of any man—the *good* that is in him! No man can know how to account for it; it is the very essence **and existence of** himself. However, in the last century they had a theory for that **too, by which it** was defined to consist in what they called *sympathies*, the necessary attraction subsisting be**tween** the inclination and the thing to be done. For all spiritual things were to be deduced from something visible and material, and thus our morality became reduced to our sympathies for others and other things.

This was the doctrine of Adam Smith and of others older than Smith, and by him this habit of morality had been termed *moral sense*, the natural relish for certain actions; a sort of palate, by the taste of which the nature of anything might be determined. Hume considered virtue to be the same as expediency, profit; that all useful things **were virtues;** that people in old times found the utility of the thing, and met, or whether they met not, in any case agreed that for the sake of keeping society together, they would patronise such things as were useful to one another, and consecrate them by some strong sanction, and that was the origin of virtue. The most melancholy theory **ever** propounded. In short, it was the highest exhibition of scepticism—that total denial of everything not material, not demonstrable by logic. The result was to convince man that he was not of Heaven,—the paltriest **conclusion.** Tell that to the savage, the red man of the forest; tell him that he **is** not of Heaven, not of God, but a mere thing of matter, and he will spurn you in his indignation at the base conclusion.

Besides morality, everything else was in the same state; all things showed what an unhealthy, poor thing the world had become. All was brought down to a system of cause and effect; of one thing pushing another thing on by certain laws of physics, gravitation, a visible, material thing of shoving. A dim, huge, immeasurable steam engine they had made of this world, and, as Jean Paul says, 'Heaven became a gas, God a force, the second world a grave.' We cannot understand how this delusion could have become so general; all men thinking in so deplorable a manner, and looking down in contempt on those who had gone before them. But it was working itself out towards issues beneficial for us all. Voltaire and Rousseau became, in the end, triumphant over everything; destroying, but substituting nothing; attacking Jesuitism, and imagining they were doing good by it; cutting down, burning up, because they were applauded for it. They had always at their back people to cry out, 'Well done!' But these having passed away, and error having once been admitted to be erroneous, and the world everywhere reduced by them to that dire condition, I say that in that huge universe, become one vast steam engine as it were, the new generation that followed must inevitably have found their position very difficult, and that it was perfectly insupportable for them to be doomed to live in such a place of falsehood and chimera. And that was, in fact, the case with them, and it led to the second great phenomenon we have to notice, the introduction of Wertherism.

Let us first look at the very centre of it, at Werther himself. 'Werther' is the first book in which there is any decided proof of its existence in the European mind. 'Werther' was written by Goethe in 1775. It was a time of a haggard condition, no genuine hope in men's minds. All outwards was false: the last war, for example, the Seven Years' War, the most absurd of wars, undertaken on no public principle, a contest between France and Germany, from Frederick the Great wanting to have Silesia, and Louis XV. wanting to give Madame de Pompadour some influence in the affairs of Europe—and 50,000 men were shot for that purpose! Under these circumstances Goethe, then of the age of twenty-five, wrote this work at Frankfort-on-Maine. A man of the liveliest imagination, and one who participated deeply in all the influences then going on, not altogether brought up in scepticism, but, in fact, very well acquainted with religious people from his youth, and, among them, with a lady named the Fraülein von Klettenberg, a follower of Zinzendorf, whom he always highly esteemed, and whom he is said to have afterwards described as the saintly lady in 'Wilhelm Meister.' But, in fact, he studied all sorts of things, and this among the rest. And when at last he grew into manhood and looked around him on what was passing, he was filled with unspeakable sadness, felt himself, as it were, flung back on himself, no sympathies in any one with his feelings, his aspirations treated as chimeras which could not realise themselves at all; and he brooded with silence long over this. He has described it all in a clear manner, a beautiful soft manner. He was destined for a profession, to be a lawyer, and though much disinclined for it he went accordingly to the University of Leipsic. Here he spent some time, till finally one of the scholars, who had been violently attached to the bride of another man, put an end to himself in despair. This gave him the idea of Werther. The sense of his own dark state and that of all others rushed upon him now more forcibly than ever, and it produced this book, the voice of what all men wanted to speak at that time, of what oppressed the heads of all, and of this young man in particular. It accordingly soon became generally read; it was translated into English among other languages. Sixty years ago young ladies here were never without all sorts of sketches on articles used at their toilettes, of Charlotte and Werther, and so on. Goethe himself was in possession of tea cups made in China ornamented with pictures of Charlotte. I suppose that the story itself is known to every one of you, yet our English version does no justice to the work. It was made, I believe, from a French translation, and it is altogether unlike the original. There is often a sharp tone, a redeeming turn of bitter satire in it, but it has become in general wearisome now to young people. It was not so in those times. Werther we may take to have been Goethe's own character, an earnest man, of deep affections, forever meditating on the phenomena of this world, and obtaining no solution, till at last he goes into sentimentality and tries that among other influences. By degrees he gets more and more desperate at his imprisonment, rages more and more against the evils around him, and at length blows his brains out, and ends the novel in that way. This was the beginning of the thing which immediately afterwards was going on through all Europe. Only till lately this country knew anything else, the thing which was not *that* was accounted no better than confusion and delusion. And they were right. *If* the world were really no better than what Goethe imagined it to be there was nothing for it but suicide. If it had nothing to support itself upon but these poor sentimentalities, view-huntings, trivialities, this world was really not fit to live in. But in the end the conviction that his theory of the world was wrong came to Goethe himself, greatly to his own profit, greatly to the world's profit.

However, this new phenomenon flamed up, and next produced 'The Robbers,' five years later than 'Werther,' a play by Schiller full of all sorts of wild things. The Robber is a student at college, kept by his brother from his inheritance, for ever moralising on the rule of life, and the conclusion he comes too is, that life is one huge Bedlam, with no rule at all, and that a brave man can do nothing with it but revolt against it. So he becomes a robber, rages and storms continually to the end of the piece, and finally kills himself, or does as good. The same sort of man as Werther, but more remarkable for that rage against the world, and the determination to alter it. Goethe says that it quite shocked him, this play of Schiller's.

There was a similar phase in the literature of our own country, if we would look at it; I allude to the works of Byron. This poet is full of indignant reprobation for the whole universe, of rage and scowl against it, as a place not worthy that a generous man should live in it. He seems to have been a compound of the Robber and Werther put together; his poems have evoked more response than any other phase of Wertherism. This sentimentalism was the ultimatum of scepticism, therefore we are bound to welcome it however absurd it may be, for it cannot be true, *that* theory of the universe; if it were, there would be no other conclusion to come to than that of Werther: to kill one's self namely—no other way for it than by one general simultaneous suicide; for all mankind to put an end to it, to return to the bosom of their fathers with a sort of dumb protest against it. There was, therefore, a deep sincerity in this sentimentalism; not a right kind of sincerity perhaps, but still a struggling towards it. We are forced to observe how like all this was to the sceptical time of Rome. That spirit raging there, in Byron and Schiller, and in Goethe's 'Werther,' trying its utmost to produce a loud noise, thinking it impossible for anything to be quiet and stormy too! So in Rome we have in her sceptical times the tragedies of Seneca, full of nothing but tumultuous rage and **storm,** ending in suicide, too, and not unreasonably either. There was no way for men but it.

But we must now pay attention to another thing which followed closely on Wertherism: another book of Goethe's, published the year after 'The Robbers,' 'Goetz von Berlichingen,' **the** subject of which was an old German baron of the time of Maximilian, grandfather of Charles V., who revoked the law of duel. Goetz, for contravening his ordinance in this, lost his right hand. A machine was made and fitted to his arm, whence he was called 'iron hand.' He was a real character, and has left memoirs of himself. This curious feature joins itself alongside of 'Werther' and 'The Robbers,' this delineation of a wild, fierce time, not as being the **sketch** of what a rude, barbarous man would appear in the eyes of a philosophical man of civilised times, but with a sort of natural regret at the hard existence of Goetz, and a genuine esteem for his manfulness and courage. By this new work Goethe began his life again; he had struck again the chord of his own heart; of all hearts. Walter Scott took it up here, too, and others. But the **charm** there is in Goethe's 'Goetz' is unattainable by any other writer. In Scott it was very good, but **by no means so good** as in 'Goetz.' It was the beginning of a happier **turn to the** appreciation of something genuine, **as** we shall notice in our next lecture. This new work, however, had come in the reign of quacks and dupes, when a good man was a kind of alien, unable to do the good that lay in him. We must accept this with a kind of cheerfulness; a system of thought, whether of belief or no belief, which results in suicide, must come to an end—that custom of judging what was right and proper in a man by the cut of his clothes, or by anything at all but the heart God had placed in him.

We come now, therefore, to the last act of scepticism, which was to sweep it all away. It was to go on but little longer; it was nearly out here too, but more so in France than elsewhere; still, a clear light enables us to trace its path. We may say that scepticism then had consummated itself. These sceptical influences had principally developed themselves on books. If they had done nothing worse, it would have been of very trifling moment. But it is the infallible result of scepticism that it produces not only bad unsound thought, but bad unsound action too. When the mind of man is sick, how shall anything about him be healthy? His conduct, too, is therefore sick, which indeed he partly feels is false himself, for there is no reality in it. The things, accordingly, that went on then reduce themselves to two; first, respect for the opinion of other people; secondly, sentimentalism. The first of these is in itself very right, but to do nothing at all without first consulting others as to whether it be moral or not, is exceedingly blameable. We say of such a man, 'all is over with that man if he is not able to be moral without help.' What is the use of always asking about morality? He has a certain light given to himself to walk by, yet he must have a great deal of talk with others about it, as if the world could keep him right by watching over him. The world will never keep him right, will never prevent him, when unseen, from breaking into doors and stealing.

The next thing, sentimentalism, plays a great part in the latter periods of scepticism. It had become necessary; it endeavoured to trace out pleasure at least in a thing where there was nothing better. The writers of this class were Rousseau, Diderot, and the rest of their school. Diderot was not at all an exemplary man, far from that: one has no business to call him virtuous at all; yet in all his books there is an endless talk about the 'pleasures of virtue,' and 'how miserable the vicious must be.' Quite as with Seneca. Then the work they made about Dilettantism, the beauties of art; an everlasting theme in that day.

In one word, there was then an universal manifestation of consciousness; every one conscious of something beautiful in himself. And that we re-remark in Werther, among others, that fine eye, the love of graceful things, which he knows he has, and thinks very desirable that other men should know it too. It is really egotism; just like a man taking out the most precious things he has in his house, and hanging them on the front wall of it, that others may see them; he himself can derive no benefit from them at all the while they are there, but only when he gets them back in his own house again. The most fatal thing in men is that recognising of their advantages, all founded in that cursed system of self-conceit; I can call it by no other name; it has never existed but for the ruin of a man.

All this went on more and more; it had gained everywhere a footing. The consequence was that men in public offices thought no more of their duties; each gave his business the go-by when he found no emolument in it. It was long since any serious attempt had been made to renovate the state of affairs. The duty was not done, though the wages were taken.

In that country, France, where scepticism was at its highest extent, we can well conceive the end of the last century, the crisis which then took place, the prurience of self-conceit, the talk of illumination, the darkness of confusion! The story of the Diamond Necklace, for example. Goethe, that remarkable character, a close observer of the French Revolution, and who understood better than any man the meaning of it, regarded this strange incident of the necklace as so much 'half-burned flax in a powder magazine!' It was but a spark amongst all this combustible matter. Such a depth of wickedness was there then in men.

Another symptom that this scepticism was about to end was the new French kind of belief—belief in the new doctrine of Rousseau, though he did not begin it. That had been already done by Mably, Montesquieu, Robertson, and other writers on what they called the *Constitution*. But Rousseau, a kind of half-mad man, but of tender pity too, struggling for sincerity through his whole life, till his own vanity and egotism drove him quite blind and desperate—Rousseau, I say, among those writers, was the first to come to the conclusion of the *Contrat Social*. But before that he wrote 'Essays on the Savage State'—that it was better to live there than in that state of society around him. We have a curious anecdote, given by himself in his 'Confessions,' of the manner in which he first formed his political opinions. He had been wandering about somewhere in the south of France, and, being very tired and hungry, he called at a cottage and asked for food. They told him they had none. He persisted in asking for some, 'were it only a crust of bread,' and at last the cottager gave him some black mouldy bread and water. He took this with thanks, spoke in a cheerful and conversible manner, and won upon the heart of his host. Whereupon the latter told him to stop, and he opened a press and took from it some extremely good food, which he set before him, telling him that he was obliged to keep very secret the possession of what comforts he had, 'or he would soon have no food for his mouth nor clothes to his back' which the king's tax-gatherer would not seize or his lord's bailiff. From that time Rousseau says he became a democrat. He began at first, as

I said, disquisitions on savage society; then followed a kind of revocation of that, a summing up of his ideas in the *Contrat Social*, the fundamental idea of the French Revolution, by which a final stop was put to the course of this scepticism, and all things came to their ultimatum.

The French Revolution was one of the frightfullest phenomena ever seen among men. Goethe, who lived in the middle of it, as it were, declared when it broke out, and for years after, he thought it 'like to sweep himself away with it, and the landmarks of everything he best knew,' into one wild black darkness and confusion. However, at last he got to know it better than any other one of his time. It was, after all, a new revelation of an old truth to this unfortunate people. They beheld, indeed, the truth there clad in hell fire, but they got the truth. This was how it ended; but it began in all the golden radiance of hope, the belief that if men would but meet and arrange in some way the Constitution, then a new heaven and new earth would come down together in this world. For they supposed that we were all arranged right enough *personally*, we only needed the arrangement of the *Constitution*. Accordingly, they arranged it in the most perfect sincerity of heart. It is impossible to doubt this sincerity. Take, for example, the Federation of 1790, undertaken in the real spirit of Fraternity, a scene of the most infantine simplicity, men falling each on the other's neck with tears of brotherly affection;

all swore that they would keep that law. All classes were rejoiced at the intelligence of this. For the upper class of people it was the joyfullest of news: now at last they had got something to *do*. To them, therefore, more even than to the lower classes, this news was joyful: certainly to *starve* to death is hard, but not so hard as to *idle* to death! These people were, therefore, glad as nation ever was: so glad! This was in 1790.

Two years and six weeks after that the September massacres began! They had never been contemplated when the Revolution commenced; no man friendly to the Revolution had any idea of it. But these people had no principle in what they did but the idea of their duty to give happiness to themselves and one another; that was their virtue. This is not a true notion of virtue. A man who would be virtuous must not expect to find happiness here. We cannot flatter him that virtue is to give him temporal happiness; it is, too often, allied to physical suffering. We can say, then, as to these phenomena of the French Revolution in general, that where dishonest and foolish people are, there will always be dishonesty and folly. We cannot distil knavery into honesty!

The next fact that we have to notice is that in such a consummation Europe would infallibly rise against it, and try to put it down. And it actually did so. Nor could Europe avoid it. Europe had a right to do what it did, just as the French Revolution, which it tried to crush, had a right to be.

For the poor people, ground down to the lowest stage of oppression and misery, had a right to rise and strive to be rid of it; they had rather be shot than endure it any longer. And Europe, which saw that this could not end with France, but that the interests of all its nations were to be transacted in that arena, had a right to put it down if it could. And there was no way to adjust these two rights except to fight it out — that dismal conclusion! Europe, therefore, assembled, and came round France, and tried to crush the Revolution, but could not crush it at all. It was the primeval feeling of nature they came to crush. Round it the old spirit of fanaticism had rallied, and it stood up and asserted itself, and made Europe know, even to the marrow of its bones, that it was there. Buonaparte set his foot on the necks of the nations of Europe.

Buonaparte himself was a reality at first, though afterwards he turned out all wrong and false. But his appreciation of the French Revolution was a good one, that it was 'the career open to talents,' not simply as Sieyès supposed, a thing consisting of two Chambers, or of one Chamber. And this, in fact, is the aim of all good government in these days, to get every good able man into action; all Europe endeavours to put the ablest man in a situation to do good. Buonaparte at last set himself up, put out the Bourbons, set up the Buonapartes. But the thing could not be done. He made wars and went about plundering everybody, and the consequence was that as all the *sovereigns* had been provoked before, France provoked every *man* now. In Germany, at last, he stirred up that old Berserker rage against him, by which he burned himself up in a day, and France then got ordered back into its own boundaries. Thus the French Revolution was only a great outburst of the truth, that this world was not a mere chimera, but a great reality. Scepticism was ended, and the way laid open to new things whenever they should offer.

In my next lecture I think I shall show you that there is a new thing; we shall see the streaks of something developing itself in Europe.

LECTURE XII.

June 11*th*.

FOURTH PERIOD.

OF MODERN GERMAN LITERATURE—GOETHE AND HIS WORKS.

During the last two or three lectures we have brought the history of that particular phenomenon of European culture, which we are obliged to denominate scepticism, down to its last manifestation, the great but not at all universally understood phenomenon of the French Revolution, the burning up of scepticism, an enormous phenomenon! It was, we saw, the inevitable consummation of such a thing as scepticism. The life of man cannot subsist on doubt or denial, it subsists only on belief, attaching itself to bring out of any particular theory what life it offers. The French Revolution began some centuries before it finally broke out; a rude condition to go through all Europe, a fiery phenomenon to go through all the world, it was indispensable. Yet, frightful as it was in itself, and as productive of a bloody twenty-five years' war, we ought to welcome it: it was the price of what is indispensable to our existence, and at that time the world at whatever price must have got done with scepticism. The human mind cannot for ever live in bitter sneering contrast with what lies about it, it must turn back at last to communion once more with Nature. It was, therefore, a cheering thing; a priceless worth was in it: by it the European family got its feet once more out of the mists and clouds of logic, and got down again to a firm footing on the ground. It is now nearly twenty-five years since the first act of this drama finished, and Napoleon, who from being the great 'armed soldier of democracy,' became at last a poor egotist, and with his ambition and rapacities provoked the whole earth, got flung out in the end to St. Helena as an instrument which Providence had once made use of, but had done with now. It becomes then interesting for us to inquire what we are to look for now. In what condition has this consummation left the minds of men? Are we to reckon on a new period of things, of better, infinitely extending hopes? or is scepticism still to go on in the same phase through Europe? To these questions we shall direct our attention to-day.

In the first place I must remark that if we admit the French Revolution to be such a thing as it really is, we shall see that such a continuance of old things had become altogether impossible, that all things predicted of it had come to pass, that men had shaken off their formulas and awoke out of the nightmare that had gone on so long, crushing the life out of them, that state of paralysis; and that man so awakened, like as in the fable of Antæus, gathered strength and life once more as he touched the earth and its realities. If we look over the history of Europe, both prior to the French Revolution and since, we see good in store for us; the political world if not better regulated still regulated by a reality, and, independently of that, the spiritual side of things undergoing a great change also, by means of the modern school in German literature, a literature presenting a character far more cheering to us than any literature that has appeared for a long series of generations.

In the second place we can notice here a striking illustration of the ancient fable of the Phœnix. The ancients had a wise meaning in all these fables, far deeper than any of their philosophies have. All things are mortal in this world; everything that exists in time exists with the law of change and mortality imprinted upon it. It is the story of the Phœnix which periodically, after a thousand years, becomes a funeral pyre of its own creation, and so out of its own ashes becomes a new Phœnix. It is the law of all things. Paganism, for example, in its time produced many great things, brave and noble men, till at last it came to fall and crumble away into a mere disputatious philosophy. And so down to the Protestant system; for the Middle Ages in this respect answered to the Heroic Ages of old Greece, and as Homer had lived, so Dante lived. Similarly the destruction of the Roman system of Paganism (for the Romans had their distinct system, very different from that of the Greeks), like the introduction of Protestantism, was followed by its own period of Wertherism, a kind of blind struggle against the evils that lay around it, and ending at last in what was infinitely more terrific than any French Revolution, that wild in-bursting of all the barbarians into the old world, long spell-bound by the Roman name, but now determined not to endure any longer the domination of so degraded and profligate a race; when, I say, these barbarians gathered themselves and burst in on that world and consumed it! The awfullest period ever known. And just so in later times the French Revolution, that bursting in of the masses who could not starve, could not submit to it, but must rise up and get rid of the oppression that weighed them down; this, I say, is little less remarkable while it lasts, until there is found force enough in society to subdue it.

These things, therefore, being finished, and lying behind us, we now naturally enough might inquire what new doctrine it is that is now proposed to us; what is the meaning of German literature? But this question is not susceptible of an immediate answer. It is one of the chief qualities of German literature, that it has no particular theory at all, in the front of it; very little theory is to be had posted there—offered for sale to us. The men who constructed the German literature had quite other objects in view; their object was not to teach the world, but to work out in some manner an enfranchisement for their own souls, to save themselves from being crushed down by the world. And on the contrary, seeing here what I have been always convinced I saw, the blessed, thrice blessed, phenomenon of men unmutilated in all that constitutes man, able to believe, and be in all things men; seeing this, I say, there is here the thing that has all other things presupposed in it. It needed but the first time to have been ever done, the second time they would have found it a great deal easier to do.

As to their particular doctrines, there is nothing definite or precise to be said. How they thought or felt, how they proposed to bring in the heroic age again, how they did their task, can only be learned by dint of studying long what it is these men found it good to say. Doubtless there are few here who are as yet sufficiently acquainted with the language to make that study, but I hope it will not be many years before it will be difficult to get any audience gathered here to hear a lecture upon the literature of Germany without having read its chief productions. To explain them best, I can only think of the revelation, for I call it no other, that these men made to me. It was to me like the rising of a light in the darkness which lay around and threatened to swallow me up. I was then in the very midst of Wertherism, the blackness and darkness of death. There was one thing in particular which struck me in Goethe: it is in his 'Wilhelm Meister.' He had been describing an association of all sorts of people of talent, formed to receive propositions and give responses to them, all which he described with a sort of seriousness at first, but with irony at the last. However, these people had long had their eye on Wilhelm Meister, with great cunning watching over him, at a distance at first, not interfering with him too soon. At last, the man who was intrusted with the management of the thing, took him in hand, and began to give him an account of how the association acted. Now this is the thing which, as I said, so much struck me. He tells Wilhelm Meister that a number of applications for advice were daily made to the association, which were answered thus and thus, but that many people wrote in particular for recipes of happiness, all that, he adds, 'was laid on the shelf, and not answered at all!' Now this thing gave me great surprise when I read it. 'What!' I said, 'is it not the recipe of happiness that I have been seeking all my life; and isn't it precisely because I have failed in finding it that I am now miserable and discontented?' Had I supposed, as some people do, that Goethe was fond of paradoxes, that this was consistent with the sincerity and modesty of the man's mind, I had certainly rejected it, without further trouble, but I could not think it. At length, after turning it over a great while in my own mind, I got to see that it was very true what he said, that it was the thing about which all the world was in error. No man has the right to ask for a recipe of happiness, he can do without happiness. There is something better than that. All kinds of men who have done great things, priests, prophets, sages, have had in them something higher than the love of happiness to guide them, spiritual clearness and perfection, a far better thing than happiness. Love of happiness is but a kind of hunger at the best; a craving, because I have not enough of sweet provision in this world. If I am asked what that higher thing is, I cannot at once make answer: I am afraid of causing mistake. There is no name I can give it that is not to be questioned. I could not speak about it: there is no name for it but Pity; for that heart that does not feel it, there is no good volition in that heart. This higher thing was once named 'The Cross of Christ,' not a happy thing *that* surely. The worship of sorrow named by the old heroic martyrs, named in all the heroic sufferings, all the heroic acts of man. I do not mean to say that the whole creed of German literature can be reduced to this one thing, it would be absurd to say so; but that was the commencement of it. And just as William Penn said of the Pagan system, that Christianity was not come to destroy what was true in it, but to purify it of errors, and then to embrace it within itself; so I began to see with respect to this world of ours, that the Phœnix was not burnt wholly up when its ashes were scattered in the French Revolution, but that there was yet something immortal in all things that were genuine, which now survived, and for the future was to cherish all hopes. For it is the special nature of man to have comfort by him, to aid and support himself. If there is any one of you here now prosecuting the same kinds of studies as I then did, and has not arrived at it yet by a way of his own (for there are many ways to it), he will, when he first discovers this high truth, be anxious to know what it is, and get better and better acquainted with it.

And that you also may be enabled to realise to yourselves what I have realised to myself, I shall proceed to point out one or two figures in German literature, one or two men who have been the chief speakers in it.

Of the philosophers of Germany, the metaphysicians of Germany, I shall say nothing at present. I studied them once attentively; but I found that I got nothing out of them. One may just say of them that they are the precisely opposite to Hume; Hume starting out of materialism and sensualism, certain of nothing except that he himself was alive; while the Germans, on the contrary, start from the principle 'that there is an universal truth in things'—spiritualism; that trying to go about seeking evidences for belief is like one who would search for the sun at noonday by the light of a farthing rushlight! Blow out your rushlight, they say, and you will soon see the sun! But this study of metaphysics, I say, had only the result, after **bringing me rapidly** through different phases **of opinion, at last, to** deliver me altogether out of metaphysics. **I found** it altogether a frothy system ; **no right** beginning to **it,** no right ending. I began with **Hume and** Diderot, and **as** long as **I was with them I ran** at Atheism, at blackness, at materialism **of all kinds.** If **I** read Kant, I arrived at **precisely** opposite **conclusions,** that **all** the world **was spirit** namely, that there was nothing material at all anywhere ; and the result was what **I have** stated, that I resolved for **my part to have** nothing more **to** do with metaphysics at all !

The first writer I shall notice **is** Goethe. The **appearance of** such a man **at** any given **era is, in my opinion,** the greatest thing that can happen in it—a man **who has the** soul to think, and be the moral **guide of** his **own** nation and of the whole **world.** All people that live under his influence gather themselves round him, and therefore, although many **writers made** their appearance **in** Germany **after** him, Goethe was the man to whom they looked for inspiration ; they took from **him the colour** they assume. I can have little **to say** of him **in these** limits. **I can** say of **him the same as I said of** Shakespeare : **there has been no such man as himself since Shakespeare.** He was not like Shakespeare, yet in some respects he came near to Shakespeare— **in his** clearness, tolerance, humane depth. He, too, was a devout man. You grant a devout man, you grant a wise man : no man has a seeing eye without first having had a seeing heart. Otherwise the genius of man is but spasmodic and frothy. I should say, therefore, that the thing one often hears, 'that such and such a man is a wise man, but a man of a base heart,' is altogether an impossibility, thank Heaven! Virtue is the palladium of our intellects. If wickedness were consistent with wisdom, we should often have the Devil in this world of ours regulating all our affairs; but the thing is impossible.

Thus all the things in Shakespeare breathe of wisdom and morality, and all are *one*. So, if you grant me Goethe's worth, you grant me all things beside it. Indeed, we may find his greatness in this one fact. We saw his 'Werther' and 'Berlichingen' appear, those fountain-heads of that European literature which has been going on ever since. Goethe himself soon got out of that altogether, and he resolved to be sincere once more, being convinced that it was all wrong, nonsense, mean, and paltry; and that, if there was nothing better to be done with it, he ought to hold his tongue about it altogether. This was to feel like one who was to become one of the kings of this world. Accordingly, for twenty years after that, while all Germany was raging, as we saw, and the whole people had in a manner become one set of desperate, whiskered manhaters, Goethe held his peace. Fame to him was little in comparison with an enfranchised soul. His next work (for 'Faust,' properly speaking, belongs to the 'Werther' period) was 'Wilhelm Meister,' published in the year 1795. This is a strange book, and though it does not fly away on the wind like 'Werther,' it is even stranger than 'Werther.'

At this time the man has got himself organized at last—built up; his mind adjusted to what he cannot cure, not suicidally grinding itself to pieces. But there was no pity yet in him. It is very curious to observe how at this time, ideal art, painting, poetry, were in his view the highest things, goodness being only included in it. There is even no positive recognition of a God, but only of a stubborn force, really a kind of heathen thing. Still, there is some belief; belief in himself, that most useful of all beliefs. He got that when his strength was at its *highest*. As his mind gets higher, more concentrated in itself (for Goethe lived very silent, the most silent of men), in its own privacy it becomes more serious too, uttering tones of most beautiful devoutness, recognitions of all things that are true in the world.

For example, in the continuation of his 'Wilhelm Meister,' written when he was near seventy years old, there is a chapter that has been called the best chapter ever yet written on Christianity. I never met anywhere with a better. It is out of that I quoted that beautiful phrase applied to Christianity, 'the Worship of Sorrow,' also styled by him 'the Divine Depth of Sorrow!' Also in the last book of all he ever wrote, the most considerable book in a poetical view, the 'West-Östlicher Divan,' we have the same display of pious feeling. Yet it is in form a Mahometan-Persian series of delineations, but its whole spirit is Christian; it is that of Goethe himself, the old poet who goes up and down singing little snatches of his own feelings on different things. It grows extremely beautiful as it goes on, full of the finest things possible, which sound like the jingling of bells when the 'queen of the fairies rides abroad.' The whole gathers itself up in the end into what Goethe thinks on matters at large. But we can see that what he spoke is not the thousandth part of what lay in him. It is, in fact, the principal charm in him, that he **has** the **wisdom** to speak what **is to be** spoken, to be silent on what is not to be spoken.

Alongside of Goethe we must rank Schiller. By-the-by, I have said nothing about the objections sometimes made to Goethe. It is a mortifying thing to feel that want **of** recognition among men **to** which a great writer is subject. **Not** that **Goethe has** not had in general **an** ample recognition; but still there are men, whose ideas are not nonentities at all, but who very much differ about Goethe and his character. One thing that has been said of him very strangely is that in all his writings he appears 'too happy.' A most amazing accusation against a man! much more against Goethe, who tells **us** that in his youth he could often have run **a dagger into** his heart. He could **at** any time have been as miserable, if **he liked,** as these critics could wish; but **he very** wisely kept his misery to himself, or rather misery was to him the problem **he** had to solve, the work **he** had to do. Thus, when somebody, on seeing his portrait, exclaimed, 'Voilà un homme qui a eu beaucoup de chagrin,' he instantly replied, 'No! but of one rather who has turned his sufferings into useful work!' Another objection made to him has been that he never took part in the political troubles of his time, never acted either as a Reformer or Conservative. But he did right not to meddle with these miserable disputes. To expect this of his genius would be like asking the moon to come out of the heavens, and become a mere street torch, and then to go out.

Schiller has been more generally admired than Goethe, and no doubt he was a noble man; but his qualification for literature was in every way narrower than Goethe's. The principal characteristic of Schiller is a chivalry of thought, described by Goethe as 'the Spirit of Freedom,' struggling ever forward to be free. It was this that produced 'The Robbers.' Goethe says that the 'very shape of his body and the air with which he walked showed the determined lover of freedom, one who could not brook the notion of slavery,' and that not only under men, but under anything else. But Schiller, notwithstanding this, in my opinion, could not have written one good poem if he had not met with Goethe. At the time of their meeting he had last written the play of 'Don Carlos,' a play full of high-sounding but startling things. The principal character, Mendoza, in particular talks very grandly and largely throughout. It is well described as being like a 'lighthouse, high, far-seen, and withal empty.' It is, in fact, very like what the people of that day, the Girondists of the French Revolution, were always talking about, the 'Bonheur du Peuple,' and the rest. To this point, then, Schiller had arrived, when, being tired of this kind of composition, he left poetry, apparently for ever, and wrote several very sound historical books, and nothing else.

Goethe, who was ten years older than Schiller, first met him at this period. He did not court an acquaintance with him. In fact, he says himself that he 'disliked Schiller,' and kept out of his way as much as possible. Schiller also disliked Goethe for his cold impassivity, and tried to avoid him too. However, they happened to come together, and a mutual friendship ensued; and it was very creditable to Schiller—how he attached himself to Goethe, and sought his instructions, and how he got light out of Goethe. There was always something, however, *monastic* in Schiller. He never attempted to bring the great page of life into poetry, but would retire into corners, and deal with it there. He was too aspiring, too restless; it brought him to the bed of sickness; he could not live in communion with earth. It is melancholy to read how in his latter days he used to spend whole nights in his garden house, drinking wine-chocolate (a beverage of which I can form no notion) to excess. Here he was often seen by his neighbours, declaiming and gesticulating and writing his tragedies. His health became completely destroyed by it, and finally he died at the age of forty.

There was a nobleness in Schiller, a brotherly feeling, a kindness of sympathy for what is true and just. There was a kind of silence, too, at the last. He gave up his *talk* about the 'Bonheur du Peuple,' and tried to see if he could *make* them happier instead. Accordingly his poems became better and better after his acquaintance with Goethe. His 'Wilhelm Tell' was the best thing he ever wrote. There runs a kind of melody through it; the description of the herdsman of the Alps is exquisite. It is a kind of Swiss thing itself; at least, there are passages in it which are quite in that character. It properly finishes at the fourth act. The fifth was afterwards added, as the rules of the drama obliged him to write it; but this, though it may have been considered a fault, is not a fault for the reader.

The third great writer in modern German literature whom I intend to notice is Jean Paul Friedrich Richter. Richter was a man of a large stature, too. He seems, indeed, to be greater than either; but, in my opinion, he was far inferior to Goethe. He was a man of a hard life, miserable enough for the people even who complain of Goethe. I do not mean that he was unhappy in any particular circumstances; but what I do say is, that he had not gained a complete victory over the world as Goethe had done. Goethe was a strong man, as strong as the mountain rocks, but as soft as the green sward upon the rocks, and, like them, continually bright and sun-beshone. Richter, on the contrary, was what he has been called, a 'half-made' man. He struggled with the world, but was never completely triumphant over it.

But one loves Richter. He is most universally to be loved, indeed, provided one can get to read him. But that is a great proviso, for his style is as confused and unintelligible, as Goethe's is the best of styles—like the clear harmony of Xenophon, but far deeper than Xenophon. As he is the best of Germans for style, Richter is the worst. He cannot get half the things said that he has to say—a confused, strange, tumultuous style! It is like some tangled American forest, where the axe has never been, and no path lies through it. For my part, I tried to understand him over and over again before I succeeded; but I got finally to perceive his way of thinking, and I found a strange kind of order in him at last, and it was quite easy after that to make him out. His is a most gorgeous style; not an articulate voice, but like the sound of cataracts falling among the wild pine forests! It goes deep in the human heart. A man of a great intellect, great heart, great character—all exemplified in his way of life.

His father, who was a clergyman, dying when he was young, left him in charge to his mother, a foolish woman, by whom his patrimony was completely wasted. In his twenty-fifth year he entered the University of Leipzig. He was at this time of a strange nature; there was a sort of affectation in him. Not only had he no words adequate to express his ideas, but those he had were not good enough. He found the professors, in his eyes, very feeble individuals. He met there, however, Ernesti, the distinguished scholar, for whom he had a great regard. Yet his college life was one of great privations. He says: 'In gaols the prisoner's allowance is bread and water. I had the latter, but not the former.' Plenty of water, but no bread! Yet he was a cheerful, indomitable man amid it all. He held his peace and struggled on, determined to wait his time. That time came! The people of the college had thought him mad, but he soon proved to them that he was not a madman, for he bestirred himself, and wrote books which became very successful. I recommend my friends here who know German to read his novels; to struggle through his difficulties of style, and get acquainted with him. He has, among other qualities, that of great joyousness; there is more joyous laughter in the heart of Richter than in any other German writer. Goethe has it to a certain extent, and Schiller too; but Richter goes into it with al his heart. It is a deep laughter, a wild laughter; and, connected with it, there is the deepest seriousness. Thus his dreams; they are as deep as those of Dante: dreams of annihilation, not surpassed, perhaps, except by the prophetic books of the Bible.

There are yet many more writers besides those

I have named, but I have not time for them. What can I do? I can but invite my friends to get acquainted with them, and find out for themselves the nature of the belief that is in these men. They will find in them not a *theory*, not the demonstration of motion; but they will see men walking, which is far better.

I shall add but a few words on our prospects of what is next to come. I think, therefore, that we have much reason to hope about the future. Great things are in store for us. The world has but begun to enter upon this new course, and wise men will, I trust, continue to come and devote themselves to it. This hope assures me when I see people in a deep distress about it; for I feel that it is possible for us to be free—to attain to the possession of a spiritual freedom, compared with which political enfranchisement is but a name; not living on any longer in a blind sensualism and egotism, but succeeding to get out and be free, out of this state of nightmare and paralysis. It is my hope that the words which were spoken by Richter in the end of the eighteenth century are to come true in this. It is a most remarkable passage, and I must endeavour to give it you. He had been saying that on the out-gates of European history he thought he could read inscribed a similar inscription to that which the Russians had engraved on the iron gate at Derbent, 'Here goes the road to Constantinople.' That so, on the out-gates of events he could also read, 'Here goes the road to virtue!' 'But as yet,' he goes on to say, 'as yet are struggles. It is now the twelfth hour of the night (it was, indeed, an awful period); birds of darkness are on the wing (evil and foul things were meditated on); the spectres uprear; the dead walk; the living dream. Thou, Eternal Providence, wilt cause the day to dawn!'

I cannot close this lecture better than by repeating these words of Richter: 'Thou, Eternal Providence, wilt cause the day to dawn!'

Nothing now remains for me but to take my leave of you—a sad thing at all times that word, but doubly so in this case. When I think of what you are and of what I am, I cannot help feeling that you have been very kind to me! I won't trust myself to say how kind! But you have been as kind to me as ever audience was to man, and the gratitude which I owe you comes to you from the bottom of my heart.

May God be with you all!

NOTES.

LECTURE I.

Page 3.—*The Pelasgi.*—Vague statements about the Pelasgi were currently and most uncritically accepted at the time of Carlyle's Lectures. Even in later years professed scholars seem unwilling to confess how little they know concerning them. Thus, a strange mixture of truth and error exists in the learned Essay of Canon Rawlinson—'On the Traditions respecting the Pelasgians'—appended to his version of Herodotus (Vol. III. pp. 530-538, 4 ed. 1880).

A useful note on the Pelasgi and some other obscure tribes mentioned by Greek writers will be found in Vol. I. of the last edition (1891) of Max Müller's *Science of Language*. After examining (p. 136 *et seq.*) the most accredited sources of information Professor Max Müller concludes—'It is lost labour to try to extract anything positive from these statements of the Greeks and Romans on the race and the language of their barbarian neighbours.'

We cannot enter here upon the discussion of a subject so wide as the origin of the Hellenic and Italic peoples. The reader will find it most compendiously treated, with abundant references to other authorities, in Vol. III. of Dr. Iwan Müller's useful *Handbuch der Klassischen Alterthums-wissenschaft*. This volume, published in 1889, is by six different authors. (It can be had separately.) No English work replaces it. For the Pelasgi see especially p. 364 and context.

Page 3.—*Foolish to War for a Woman.*—'Now as for the carrying off of women, it is the deed, they say, of a rogue; but to make a stir about such as are carried off, argues a man a fool.

Men of sense [*e.g.*, Ulysses, in Shakespeare's *Troilus and Cressida*] care nothing for such women, since it is plain that without their own consent they would never be forced away. The Asiatics, when the Greeks ran off with their women, never troubled themselves about the matter; but the Greeks, for the sake of a single Lacedæmonian girl, collected a vast armament, invaded Asia, and destroyed the kingdom of Priam.' Herodotus, I. 4 (Rawlinson's version). Io and Europé are noticed in the preceding paragraphs 1 and 2.

Page 6.—*Greek still spoken in parts of Italy.*—The following passage lately written at Lecce (Lupiæ) in southern Italy by a well-known French poet and romance-writer eloquently confirms Carlyle's words :—

'Un je ne sais quoi de délicat s'y mêle qui trahit, par-dessous l'Italie et l'Espagne, le vieux fond Hellène. Dans cette province peuplée de villages où l'on parle encore grec, il semble qu'un rien de l'âme antique ait laissé partout sa trace. Les airs que chantent les enfants prennent déjà ce traînement de mélopée grave, très distinct de la cantilène si vite commune de Naples. Les habitants ont une sobriété de gestes qui contraste avec le voisinage du Midi bruyant. Il y a, dans le détail des choses de la rue, des gentillesses où l'on se plait à retrouver la preuve d'une race affinée,—comme ce petit pont de bois monté sur des roues que l'on dresse d'un trottoir à l'autre par les jours de pluie pour que vous puissiez passer sans vous salir,—et, lorsque c'est comme maintenant, marché public, la forme des lampes de terre avec leur bec allongé, celle des vases, j'allais dire des amphores, ménagées pour l'huile et le vin, avec leurs deux oreilles, suffit à vous rappeler que ces paysans venus des plaines avoisinantes sont les héritiers modernes des colons crétois débarqués avec Idoménée et les arrière-neveux des anciens sujets de Daunus, le beau-père de Diomède.' (Paul Bourget, *Sensations d'Italie*, p. 220. Paris, 1891.)

Page 7.—*Date of the Trojan War.*—For 'a list of the principal views on this subject' see Rawlinson's note to Herodotus, II. 145.

NOTES.

Page 8.—*Lycidas.*—Herodotus, IX. 5.

Page 10.—*Pelasgic Architecture.*—Usually termed Cyclopean. See Rawlinson's **Herodotus**, Vol. III. p. 537 ; 4 ed. See also *Schliemann's Ausgrabungen,* von Dr. Carl Schuchhardt, 2 ed. Leipzig, 1891. This useful book, epitomising in one volume all Schliemann's works, is now translated into English. The wall of Tiryns, figured on p. 122, has many stones measuring 2–3 metres in length, and 1 metre (nearly forty inches) in height and depth.

Page 11.—*Euhemerism.*—For a satisfactory explanation of this theory on the origin of mythology see **Max** Müller's *Science of Language,* Vol. II. p. 449, ed. of 1891.

Page 13.—*Philippides.*—His name in many manuscripts is spelt—Pheidippides. Herodotus, VI. 105.

Page 14.—*The Getæ.*—Herodotus, IV. 94. The other people who made **war** upon the south wind are the Psylli (Herodotus, IV. 173), noticed by Plutarch, Pliny, and various writers. They lived close to the Greater Syrtis, in the Libyan oases, and were renowned as snake-charmers.

LECTURE II.

Page 17.— *Wolff.*—Many do not know that the opinions on Homer which have made the name **of Friedrich August Wolf** so celebrated were anticipated **by Giambattista** Vico, the author of the *Scienza Nuova,* of whose life and writings **a pleasing** account, by Bishop **Thirlwall,** will be found in the second volume of the *Philological Museum* **(Cambridge,** 1833).

Page 17.—*The Homeric Controversy.*—What is called the Homeric question has two divisions. Both concern the Iliad. The first compares this poem with the Odyssey. The second discusses the relations of the whole Iliad to its parts.

Many passages of the Odyssey, considered (as Hamlet says) too curiously, seem to **show** that it may have been composed at a later period than the Iliad. It describes scenes and beliefs, men, arts, and circumstances, in a manner often foreign to our readings of its predecessor. These views, respectable when urged by thoughtful critics, have gained a crowd of adherents to the opinion—that one Homer could not have written both poems, an opinion older than the Christian era.

That the Iliad, as we now have it, is without unity of composition has certainly not yet been proved. Wolf's conglomerate theory, to which so many have yielded (it may be with reservations put forward as critical by those who envy Wolf his miserable reputation), appears allowable only so long as we dwell on the mosaic structure of the poem with its varied episodes and its few trifling inconsistencies. Let us grant that before Wolf's time this mixed nature of the Iliad was not sufficiently recognised (for Homer's changes are so pleasing that one pauses not always to ask the reasons of these changes). Is the Iliad therefore a patchwork, because we cannot believe in a Homer who invented all that was once assigned him and who was supposed himself to supply his own materials? The rhapsodists living before and beside Homer doubtless recited numerous hymns and ballads, the greatest of which told the fate of Troy and the anger of Achilles. They sang to audiences who appreciated the diverse versions of their lays due to the inventiveness of successive singers. Homer, his mind filled with these songs, re-shaped and put together such of them as best fitted his high purpose. In this work of giving form and combination to scattered themes lay the real strength of his genius. Could any poet do more? The elements of existence are always the same; the artist moulds and composes them into expressiveness. The infinite lies ever around us, within us. The commonest things are more suggestive than we suppose; they are infinite in the extent and diversity of their relationships.

The whole Homeric question thus gets involved in the wider one concerning the application of current phrases to designate the artist's productions. What is the significance of words like invention and originality, employed as synonyms for a certain excellence of literary compositions? The word invention itself, by a happy amphibolism, when used transitively cannot be deprived of its primitive meaning. Shakespeare knew this. He represents Worcester planning the rebellion against Henry IV., but he makes Falstaff say of him with grim irony, 'Rebellion lay in his way, and he found it.' Poor Worcester therefore was not original, though his invention cost him his head. No man of genius is original if we regard only his materials. A weaver is nobody. A smith makes neither coals nor iron ore. The miner who is nearer nature is an extractor, not a fabricator. Such spurious analysis would render Saxo, not Shakespeare, the author of Hamlet; it would resolve portraits into pigments and canvas. But who accepts these results? True invention is a thing too subtle to be analysed. The critics who like parasites crawl over men of genius never can discover it. On the other hand there is a painful originality which all excellent authors avoid. They remember that what is called the commonplace interests when presented from new points of view. The overpowering inventiveness of Edgar Poe is a defect; his horrors displease us on a second perusal. Sophocles, more moving than any other tragedian except the author of 'Lear,' did not invent the awful myth of Œdipus. He took it as it was and transformed it for ever into a thing of power and beauty. The story of the Saltzburg emigrants was re-fashioned by Goethe into his 'Hermann und Dorothea.' Art and nature, here in perfect harmony, have united to produce the most finished, the most Greek-like of post-classical poems. The first, like the last, of poets was a shaper, a creator. Before all others he called into being persons and deeds never to be forgotten. The real Agamemnon must have been a poor creature compared to the 'King of Men' portrayed by Homer.

In reviewing Homer it is wrong to begin by contrasting the Iliad with the Odyssey—an easy task. This was Wolf's procedure, who did but industriously follow a clue already traced in the writings of Bentley. By pursuing an opposite course, by first studying the Iliad as an independent work, we drop the prejudice which makes plausible these attempts to break the earlier epic into pieces. If then we again take up the Odyssey we find it not so difficult to conclude that its author also wrote the Iliad. To retain the more archaic constituents of the latter was surely **not** beyond Homer's skill. The remembrance of old customs and of quaint phrases **had** not yet expired in the minds of **his hearers.** The nice discrimination **of the means** at his **disposal** for the proper treatment **of his** two great subjects **could not puzzle** Homer, as it **has** done his **commentators.**

Homer is for laymen more than for scholars. These have **mauled** him and **made** a muddle of **his** works, his fame, his **personality;** those **have** revered him and above all read him. **They have** translated his writings, **excavated** his soil, and drawn renewed inspiration from his surroundings. **Voss** and Lord Derby, Schliemann and Byron have interpreted **Homer** better even than Heyne, better than the learned and conscientious Grote. Schliemann's diggings have caused us to distrust Grote's excessive scepticism, so gently rebuked by his friend Hallam (whose long letter is given in *The Personal Life of George Grote*, by Mrs. Grote, pp. 164–169). Byron's plea for the truth of Homer now triumphantly shows (see his 'Bride of Abydos,' Canto II., 2–4) that the poet's insight transcends that **of the** professors. All difficulties about the Homeric poems sink into **nothing** when **we grasp the final question—could a plurality of Homers** have **existed ?** That they did not exist is **a belief some** students have never ceased to cherish. And (to borrow Yorick's words) ' the vulgar are of the same opinion to this hour.'

Page 19.—*Robin Hood's Ballads*.—A much better illustration is now afforded by the *Kalevala* of the Tavastians or inhabitants of Western Finland. 'Their epic songs still live among the poorest, recorded by oral tradition alone, and preserving all the features of a perfect metre and of a more ancient language. A national feeling has arisen amongst **the Fins,** despite of Russian supremacy: and the labours of Sjögern, Lönnrot, Castrén, Kellgren, Krohne, **and Donner,** receiving hence a powerful impulse, **have** produced **results** truly surprising. From **the mouths of the** aged **an epic poem** has been collected equalling the *Iliad* **in length** and completeness—nay, if we can forget for a moment all that we in our youth learned to call beautiful, not less beautiful. A Fin is not a Greek, and

Wainamoïnen was not a Homeric rhapsodos. But if the poet may take his colours from that nature by which he is surrounded, if he may depict the men with whom he lives, **the** *Kalevala* possesses merits not dissimilar from those of the *Iliad*, and will claim its place as the fifth national epic of the world, side by side with the Ionian songs, with the [Indian] *Mahâbhârata*, the [Persian] *Shâhnâmeh*, and the [German] *Nibelunge*. If we want to study the circumstances under which short ballads may grow up and become amalgamated after a time into a real epic poem, nothing can be more instructive than the history of the collection of the *Kalevala*. We have here facts before us, not mere surmises, as in the case of the Homeric poems and the Nibelunge. We can still see how some poems were lost, others were modified; how certain heroes and episodes became popular, and attracted and absorbed what had been originally told of other heroes and other episodes. Lönnrot could watch the effect of a good and of a bad memory among the people who repeated the songs to him, and he makes no secret of having himself used the same freedom in the final arrangement of these poems which the people used from whom he learnt them.' (Max Müller's *Science of Language*, Vol. I., p. 437.)

Page 20.—*Character of Homer's Poems.*—Homer in describing natural objects and events had the advantage over other eminent poets of coming first. But this will not account for his inimitable freshness. Neither can we explain it by saying that he possessed those qualities which all consummate artists share in common. To feel the full charm of Homer we must hear him as a Greek who sung to Greeks. That is why he is now addressing the world.

The adaptation of Greek character to Greek circumstances supplies a constant topic for admiration. Greece so suited the ancient Greeks during the earlier and better periods of their history that one might say truly—mind has never since been so happily combined with matter. English readers, a few students and visitors to the Mediterranean excepted, seem to miss the significance of Greece through some vice or defect of organization. Yet one may still walk up to the Acropolis through the ' shining clear air' of Euripides. Fogs and beer are but poor substitutes for wine and sunlight. The English, though wealthy and powerful, are discontented. The Greeks were active but not unresting as we are. Disposed to cheerfulness they gained repose by not craving what was beyond their reach. The Greeks loved returning to familiar things; they sought no impossible pleasures, but enjoyed life as they found it amid their own beautiful world. Mountains to them were awful as the dwelling-places of the gods, yet they saw these mountains arising from pleasant plains and rearing their crests under a smiling heaven. Ever the blue sky covered them, the earth was fertile, the forest-shade grateful, the sea rich and strange, the air fragrant, luminous, and warm. The Greek mind was fitted by a wonderful capacity to take in all the good it could get. Like flowers on a fine day, this gay intellectual people opened to receive the light that shone on them. Their feelings did not wear out. Their senses did not tire. They did not, like the moderns, faint from *ennui*. Unlike the cold inhabitants of Northern Europe, the demon of dissatisfaction had not taken possession of their souls. Pessimist critics fail to perceive the inherent excellence of the Greeks. Their learning alone will not teach them to appreciate these children of the sun who, with child-like susceptibility, thought daily existence a delight, who *lived* and who were happy. Pleased with so much gratitude the whole universe looked on; kind Nature smiled and flung fresh gifts to the favoured of earth and heaven. Thus Art arose, a bright exhalation of the dawn, a grateful incense upon Nature's altar. What the Greek saw he loved, what he wrought he refined, what he touched he made beautiful. His thoughts were, like his firmament, transparent, exquisite; his works sincere, fair, and finished. Why did he not stay with us? Why did he go away to a heaven always rich and leave an earth made poor without him? 'The Beauty asked Zeus—why am I so transitory? Did I not, said the god, make only the transitory fair?' These are the words of one who well understood the Greeks, though he was a modern and a German. But he was a man of genius and a poet—Goethe. Happily genius is beyond time and place. Let us pray that men of genius may ever arise to console mankind for the absence of the vanished Greeks.

Goethe has a striking passage in his Propyläen showing why a perfect work of Art appears also like a work of Nature. He says—'It is *supra naturam*, but not *extra naturam*. A perfect work of Art is a creation of the human mind, and in this sense it is also a work of Nature. But whereas the scattered parts are here gathered up into one, and even to the most insignificant are assigned their due import and dignity, on that account does it rank above Nature. In conception, and composition, it is the creation of a mind which, by origin and cultivation, is at harmony with itself; and such a mind finds that by nature it is in unison with all that is intrinsically excellent and perfect.' [Shakespeare comes close to these views in Act IV., Scene 3, of *A Winter's Tale*.]

Moreover the modesty of the artist, who knows better than others that he cannot comprehend the full suggestiveness of his subject, makes him appear less than he is. Carlyle has profoundly said—'In the commonest human face there lies more than Raphael will take away with him.' The true artist therefore gives us his thoughts under the guise of simple descriptions.

Such are Homer's descriptions. His words convey more than they first express. They never lose their meaning. They still speak to us when the battle of life is well nigh over. Eminent men of noisy reputation, once innocent scholars but led astray by worldly ambition (whether on the paths of politics, law, trade, or ecclesiastical strife matters little), may keep uncorrupted one corner of their heart which registers and responds to youthful sympathies with Homer. Such men cannot be altogether lost. There is a something in them, if not their own, which may yet soften the inexorable Parcæ, nay even Minos himself. Plutarch tells how the Sicilians, before sheltering a ship chased by pirates, asked if any on board could repeat to them verses from Euripides.

Page 21.—*Poseidon.*—It was at the Isthmian games that Poseidon was especially honoured. In less pious times a profane Greek versifier thus referred to him :—

> 'When Neptune appeared at the Isthmian games,
> He spoke most politely to numerous dames.

> But, not finding one free from frivolity,
> He bowed and went back to his home in the sea.
> "The mermaids," he murmured, "are better for me."'

Pausanias (VIII., 10) tells how 'the Mantineans said that Poseidon appeared helping them' in their victory over the Lacedæmonians (see Mr. Shilleto's translation).

Page 22.—*The Dark-coloured Sea.*—In his beautiful passage on art (Iliad, XXIII., 313–318, and context) Homer makes Nestor say to Antilochus—

> 'By skill the steersman guides
> His flying ship across the dark-blue sea.'

Dark-blue is here Lord Derby's translation of a word which, strictly rendered, is *wine-looking*. (The French call certain dark-coloured wines *vins bleus*.) The Latin translators of Homer ventured to substitute *black*. Homer has another term for the open sea reflecting the light blue of the sky. The sea 'far shaded by the rocky shore' (Byron's 'Giaour,' line 43) and dangerous to the pilot was what Nestor meant. The fine and almost weird effect produced by this dark water in contrast with 'the blue crystal of the seas' beyond (*ibid*, line 17) and the intense brightness of the firmament much impressed Goethe when for the first time he saw it at Palermo (the scenic character of Sicily resembling that of Greece rather than Italy). Byron must have been very familiar with it, and Lord Derby, with appreciative tact, probably thought he could not do better than follow the lines in the 'Bride of Abydos' (Canto I., 9)—

> 'His head was leant upon his hand,
> His eye look'd o'er the dark blue water.'

Other English translators (see Walker's *Clavis Homerica*, p. 47) say *the darkling main*, which sounds affected and is erroneous, the appearance referred to being no characteristic of the ocean in general. Homer was not thinking of the main, but of those parts of the Mediterranean which had often charmed him. I do not know whether Mr. Ruskin has noted this passage.

Some German critics interpret *wine-looking* differently. Thus Göbel thinks it means transparent as opposed to troubled sea-water. Autenrieth restricts it to the deep open sea, when it reflects light in calm warm weather (see the *Lexicon Homericum* edited by H. Ebeling). It seems to be forgotten that deep water may occur very close to shore. Homer applies this word eighteen times to the sea, twice to cattle. Drs. Butcher and Lang translate it in both cases *wine-dark*.

Page 23.—*Epithets of Ulysses*.—The endurance, or rather pale rage, of Ulysses against the suitors is perhaps best shown in the opening of Book XX. of the Odyssey. Ulysses, after nightfall, has gone to rest on a bed of skins in the verandah of his own house. Seeing the suitors' mistresses go by his wrath is stirred, whereupon he displays the struggle within his mind by alternately expressing and calming his pent-up feelings. The reader is referred to the translation of the Odyssey by Drs. Butcher and Lang, the best English prose version known to us. These writers for *much-enduring* substitute *steadfast*.

As to the epithets of Ulysses Carlyle is certainly wrong. The word he translated by the phrase—'man of cunning and stratagem' (*i.e.*, prudent, strategic) is applied to Ulysses only fourteen times in the Iliad, but sixty-six times in the Odyssey. It has three approximate synonyms, similarly used, eight times in the former, twenty-four in the latter poem. The term much-enduring, with its synonyms, does not occur in the Odyssey fifty times. Surely the two qualities Carlyle opposes are not incompatible. They are so far from being so that Homer himself ascribes both to his hero in the context of the passage to which we have above referred. If Victorian is to prevail over Elizabethan English the terms *canny* and *gritty* will take the places of prudent and steadfast.

Page 25.—*Ajax like an Ass*.—Homer's comparison of Ajax to an ass may be *naïf*, but it is also scientifically true and simply excellent.

'As when a sluggish ass has got the better of the boys,
Passing by a harvest field, and many a stick is broken
Upon him, yet he gets within and crops the lofty corn,
While they with cudgels smite him, yet their strength cannot avail,
And hardly is he driven forth when satisfied with food.'
            Iliad, XI., 558–562.

The ass, like Ajax, is constitutionally courageous to a very high degree. Not being a predacious animal, it shows its courage chiefly in defence, as Ajax does in the passage quoted. The strong nervous system of the ass is displayed not only by its pertinacity but by its soundness; for, in spite of the bad treatment it receives, it is little subject to those disorders of wind and limb which beset the horse. Moreover, in southern and eastern countries the domestic ass is often a splendid animal, carefully improved by selection. In Homer's days such selection was not unknown. The wild ass is as graceful as the gazelle. In England the ass appears abject, since it suffers from the poverty or ignorance of its owner. See on this point what is said by Darwin in his *Variation of Animals and Plants under Domestication*. In Carlyle's younger days little attention was paid to those extra-zoological topics which concern rather the scholar than the naturalist, and which are now made familiar to us by the writings of De Gubernatis, Victor Hehn, and others. Gibbon, it is true, urged historical students to read for pleasure and profit those classical chapters of Buffon which describe domestic animals. Buffon nobly pleads for the ass, neglected by the narrow-minded merely because it is not a horse.

Page 25.—*The Greek type.*—The late Mr. Hope, in his *Anastasius* (Chap. IV.), puts into the mouth of a modern Greek the following reflections on his countrymen:—

'Believe me, the very difference between the Greeks of time past and of the present day arises only from their thorough resemblance; from that equal pliability of temper and of faculties in both, which has ever made them receive with equal readiness the impression of every mould and the impulse of every agent. When patriotism, public spirit, and pre-eminence in arts, science, literature, and warfare, were the road to distinction, the Greeks shone the first of patriots, of heroes, of painters, of poets, and of philosophers. Now that craft and subtlety, adulation and intrigue, are the only paths to greatness, these same Greeks are—what you see them!'

See the context. *Anastasius* was at first attributed to

Lord Byron, who in the earlier pages of his 'Giaour' severely lashes the degenerate Greeks. For an eloquent tribute to the qualities of the ancient Greeks consult the *Port-Royal* of Sainte-Beuve (Livre 3, xviii.).

Page 27.—*Pythagoras.*—Bayle in his article on this philosopher cites almost all of the classical comments on the precept as to abstinence from beans. A further copious instalment of Pythagorean literature is given in Krug's *Encyclopädisch-philosophisches Lexicon*.

Page 31.—*Æschylus.*—A spirited translation into English verse of the opening chorus of the Agamemnon was published in the *Classical Museum* (Vol. VII., pp. 97–104) by Professor Blackie, who wrote several useful papers on Æschylus in earlier volumes of the same periodical.

Page 32.—*Sophocles.*—Those who wish to enjoy and understand Sophocles should use the editions and translations of his plays now being revised by Professor Jebb. Cambridge has at length the honour of being foremost to interpret this, the foremost of the Greek dramatists, as formerly she took possession of Euripides by means of his two illustrious editors, separated from each other by a century—Barnes and Porson.

Page 33.—*Socrates.*—The reader of course is aware that we possess no writings of Socrates, and that what we know of him is chiefly derived from reports of his conversation and habits by Xenophon and Plato. These rank among the most precious and pleasing of the Greek prose classics. A very readable account of Socrates was given by Bishop Hampden in his 'Fathers of Greek Philosophy' (reprinted from the *Encyclopædia Britannica*). The reader may consult this as a corrective (especially pp. 403 *et seq.*) of Carlyle's remarks on Socrates as a wire-drawer. The prejudice of Carlyle against our philosopher was noticed by Emerson when he visited Carlyle in 1833,—'We talked of books. Plato he does not read, and he disparaged Socrates.' Besides a paper by Schleiermacher 'On the Worth of Socrates as a Philosopher' (translated by Bishop Thirlwall in Vol. II. of the *Philological Museum*) the most important works on Socrates are Grote's *Plato* and *La Philosophie de Socrate*, par Alfred Fouillée, 2 vols., Paris, 1874.

Page 35.—*The Greek decline.*—For a compendious survey of the Greek authors neglected by Carlyle see Jebb's *Primer of Greek Literature*, a book equally profitable to young and old students, particularly Part III., 'The Literature of the Decadence.' Also, *Geschichte der Byzantinischen Litteratur*, von Karl Krumbacher. 8vo., München, 1891.

LECTURE III.

Page 39.—*The Etruscans.*—More copious and accurate information on this people, whose real origin is conjectural and whose language is still completely isolated, may be had from K. O. Müller, *Die Etrusker*, 2 Aufl., von Deecke, Stuttgart, 1876, 1877.

Page 40.—*Cato, Varro* and *Columella.*—David Hume gives some interesting references to these writers in his Essay XI., ' Of the Populousness of Ancient Nations.'

Cicero (*De Senectute*, XV.) represents M. Porcius Cato vindicating at length the claims of agricultural pursuits as well fitted to occupy the energies of the Romans.

Page 45.—*Napoleon on Hannibal.*—The following citation is from the *Mémorial de Sainte-Hélène*, of Las Cases (Tome VII., p. 237):—

'Et cet *Annibal*, disait-il, le plus audacieux de tous, le plus étonnant peut-être; si hardi, si sûr, si large en toutes choses; qui, à 26 ans, conçoit ce qui est à peine concevable, exécute ce qu'on devait tenir pour impossible; qui, renonçant à toute communication avec son pays, traverse des peuples ennemis ou inconnus qu'il faut attaquer et vaincre, escalade les Pyrénées et les Alpes, qu'on croyait insurmontables, et ne descend en Italie qu'en payant de la moitié de son armée la seule acquisition de son champ de bataille, le seul droit de combattre; qui occupe, parcourt et gouverne cette même Italie durant 16 ans, met plusieurs fois à deux doigts de sa perte la terrible et redoutable Rome, et ne lâche sa proie que quand on met à profit la leçon qu'il a donnée d'aller le combattre chez lui. Croira-t-on qu'il ne dut sa carrière et tant de grandes actions qu'aux caprices du hasard, aux faveurs de la fortune ? Certes, il devait être doué d'une forte trempe d'âme, et avoir une bien haute idée de sa science ; en guerre, celui qui, interpellé par son jeune vainqueur, n'hésite pas à se placer, bien que vaincu, immédiatement après Alexandre et Pyrrhus, qu'il estime les deux premiers du métier.' Napoleon further comments on Hannibal in his ' Notes sur l'Art de la Guerre.' (See *Correspondance de Napoléon 1er*, Tome XXXI. Paris, 1869.)

Page 47.—*Words traced to the Pelasgi.*—For 'sufficient proof that Latin never could have passed through the Greek, or what used to be called the Pelasgic stage, but that both are independent modifications of the same original language ' see Vol. I. of Max Müller's *Science of Language*.

Page 52.—*Ovid.*—Carlyle would perhaps have been less severe on Ovid had he noted that the grave Milton preferred the 'Metamorphoses' of this poet to any other of the Latin classics. Barrow also is loud in his praise. The elder Rousseau thus sums him up,—

> ' Ovide, en vers doux et mélodieux,
> Sut débrouiller l'histoire de ses dieux :
> Trop indulgent au feu de son génie,
> Mais varié, tendre, plein d'harmonie,
> Savant, utile, ingénieux, profond,
> Riche, en un mot, s'il était moins fécond.'

The moralising Seneca abused him. Montaigne failed to appreciate him. *Principes poetæ Virgilius et Ovidius* is the verdict of Joseph Scaliger. But he thought the Epistles of Ovid his most perfect work.

Page 57.—*Passage from Tacitus.*—Of this passage, celebrated as the first noteworthy reference to the early Christians by a pagan author, Gibbon (*Decline and Fall*, Chap. XVI.) gives another translation.

The same passage is further remarkable as showing how Tacitus sometimes loses power by not considering that the law of moderation holds good even in the exercise of that rare merit—brevity of expression. Further illustrations of this defect in that great writer are pleasantly discussed by Father Bouhours in his delightful *Manière de Bien Penser dans les Ouvrages d'Esprit*, a book which, together with the Memoirs of Cardinal de Retz, was highly commended by the most graceful of English politicians, Lord Chesterfield.

LECTURE IV.

Page 58.—*The Middle Ages.*—The recognition of the Middle Ages shows that tripartite arrangements, in spite of superficial objections, are not always to be set aside in favour of more popular and usually more logical binary divisions. The partition of history into ancient and modern is less intelligible and significant. Perhaps, when the world is older, this partition may come to be adopted; but in that case what we call the Middle Ages will then be relegated to ancient history, and modern history will date from the first appearance of printed books, or from the nearly coincident epoch of the discoveries of Columbus.

The breaking-up of the Roman Empire was a slow process. Until it begins we are clearly within the limits of ancient history. But when did it begin? Roman decadence came not alone from invading barbarians, becoming conscious of their growing power. It was also promoted from within. It had its origin while the empire yet appeared strong, but displayed its self-abasement by allowing its seat to be transferred from the banks of the Tiber to those of the Bosphorus.

The Middle Ages end with the Byzantine Empire. But this empire had long before become insignificant, though not till long after were established those European kingdoms whose foundation seemed to follow the failure of the great Roman dominion. Are these modern kingdoms established? Greece was reconstituted during the first half of our century; Italy in the second half. To the present boundaries of the German empire a date of less than a quarter of a century can be assigned. And now we hear of wars threatening again to unfix these limits. An ironical writer might say, not without truth, that the beginnings of modern history are still dubious, and that their adequate consideration must be left to some historian yet unborn.

For the present, however, we may conveniently distinguish the Middle Ages (330-1453) as exhibiting (a) a capital city, (b) a religion, (c) certain forms of government, (d) a learned language, and (e) a poem, which differs no less from the literary productions of antiquity than it does from those of modern times.

(a.) Constantinople was the capital city of the Middle Ages, which began with its dedication by Constantine, and ended with its capture by the Turks. Here again comes in the irony of events. In ancient history Europe triumphs over Asia; the Trojans, the Persians, the Phœnicians, and others being in turn successfully repelled. While modern history is introduced by the establishment in Europe of an Asiatic power, which holds possession of the seat of mediæval rule to this day.

(b.) The religion of the Middle Ages in Europe was Catholicism, i.e., established Christianity. Constantine's endowment of his own Church could not hinder the split which afterwards severed the eastern from the western Christians. It is easy to exaggerate the importance of this schism, which served to show that Rome, deprived of temporal sway, could still subdue the minds of men. The blow dealt the Catholic Church by the secession of northern Europe from its allegiance marks indeed the commencement of modern history. Yet was this loss the effect of printing and political causes rather than of sincere religious convictions, and the Papal power has since succeeded in checking the further advances of Protestantism.

(c.) As to government, the Middle Ages display the downfall of despotism, the anarchy which ensued, and the subsequent rise of feudal authority. The peoples of Europe then possessed very little power. The Roman pontiffs became more dominant than kings or emperors. Subject to qualification the general proposition is true—that monarchy, oligarchy, and democracy, respectively, characterise the three great periods of history. In this matter likewise we seem (but seem only) returning to ancient ways.

(d.) During the transitional linguistic conditions of the Middle Ages men of learning found a temporary aid in such

Latin as they could use, good, bad, and indifferent. The *Glossarium* of Du Cange remains the most indispensable guide to the Middle Ages in the hands of those who know how to read it.

(*e.*) But in 1300 a bold, though not unconsidered, way of escape from this prevailing influence of the Latin language was indicated by no less a person than **Dante**. Not only does the **Divine Comedy reveal** the Middle Ages and Catholicism by a crowd of allusions, else lost to us, but its unapproachable excellence of diction makes welcome the light it sheds on what is eternal in man's nature, and those recurring events which to the serious never can lose their significance.

Much labour will henceforth be spared the student of the Middle Ages who has at hand the valuable *Trésor de Chronologie d'Histoire et de Géographie pour l'étude et l'emploi des documents du Moyen Age,* par M. le Cte De Mas Latrie, Paris, 1889.

Page 61.—*Belief during the Middle Ages.*—Jean Paul in his eulogium of Herder has these words (which we give from the translation of De Quincey):—

'Two sayings of his survive, which may seem trifling to others; me they never fail to impress profoundly: one was, that on some occasion, whilst listening to choral music that streamed from a neighbouring church as from the bosom of some distant century, he wished, with a sorrowful allusion to the cold frosty spirit of these times, that he had been born in the Middle Ages.'

Page 67.—*The Celebrated Letter of Pliny.*—The reader may compare this letter with Trajan's reply in the *Letters of the Younger Pliny*, translated by J. T. Lewis, London, 1879 (p. 377).

Page 70.—*Pope Hildebrand.*—For a careful and unprejudiced history of this great reformer, with abundant references to other authorities, see *Hildebrand and his Times* by the Rev. W. R. W. Stephens, London, 1888; a small but useful book. In the Homily against Disobedience and wilful Rebellion some violent abuse of Hildebrand will be found.

Page 73.—*The Crusades.*—Considerate historians now believe that the two great lessons taught by the crusades were these.—First, the more thoughtful crusaders learnt that eastern infidels, Jews, Turks and heretics might be as good as themselves, and that sometimes it is right to regard our conduct towards our neighbours from points of view which priests are apt to neglect. Next, the citizens of western Europe, left to themselves, found they could do very well without feudalism. Thus the air was cleared, and people began to see how their freedom from licensed robbers, whether of land, power or privilege might, perhaps, one day be accomplished.

Page 75.—*The Troubadours.*—Our best guides to the language and literature of the Troubadours are still the works of Fr. Raynouard, who was, however, wrong in regarding Provençal as the mother, rather than the sister, of French and other modern Romance languages. His *Choix des poésies originales des Troubadours* is indispensable. Taylor's *Lays of the Minnesingers and Troubadours* may also be noted. Useful are the *Essays on Petrarch* by Ugo Foscolo. According to Coleridge, 'Petrarch was the final blossom and perfection of the Troubabours.' The Italian text of Dante's Purgatorio is curiously interrupted (close of Canto XXVI.) by eight lines of Provençal, spoken by the once-famous poet Arnaud.

Page 76.—*The Niebelungen Lied.*—Carlyle's review of Simrock's edition of the Nibelunge, reprinted among his *Miscellanies*, should of course be consulted. It is full of information and contains some very striking specimens of his powers as a translator.

LECTURE V.

Page 80.—*The Lombards.*—The etymology of their name endorsed by Carlyle is now questioned. Longobardi may mean (not *long beards*, but) those living *along the border* of the Elbe, whence the Lombards are supposed to have come. See a note by Dr. William Smith to Vol. V., p. 165 of his edition of Gibbon.

As to Magna Græcia (mentioned in the same page) most interesting details are given by Fr. Lenormant, *La Grand Grèce—Paysages et Histoire* (3 tomes, Paris, 1881-1884). But see further the remarks in Vol. III. (p. 474) of Dr. Iwan Müller's *Handbuch*, to which work we have referred in our Notes to Lecture I.

Page 81.—*Illustrious Italians.*—Desiring to occupy most of his lecture with Dante, Carlyle says nothing of the two great poets, Tasso and Ariosto. England has had the honour of publishing the best edition of both Orlandos (that of Ariosto and his predecessor Boiardo), by the learned Panizzi. Neither does he mention the Italian historians. On these two topics much that is valuable is told us by Isaac D'Israeli in his *Curiosities of Literature*, first and second series.

Carlyle can scarcely be blamed for not anticipating the advent of another group of Italian worthies, including those heroic or more thoughtful men of action, such as Garibaldi and Cavour, who have so unselfishly achieved the noble work of liberating their country.

Page 85.—*Æschylus, Dante, Shakespeare.*—Many will demur to this juxtaposition and say that the greatest poet of antiquity was Homer, of the Middle Ages Dante, and of modern times Goethe; Shakespeare being 'not for an age, but for all time.' Truly Æschylus is grand, but he is not the representative poet of Greece, like Homer.

Page 86.—*Quotations from Dante.*—To understand these quotations we must remember that the Inferno really consists of three unequal regions. The first of these, outside Dante's first circle, from which it is separated by the river Acheron, is for the *frivolous*, those mean Laodicean souls who are neither cold nor hot. The first circle, also called Limbo, is the place of the *sinless unbaptized*. It includes good pagans, many infants, and others. The remaining eight circles are for *unrepentant sinners*. The incontinent occupy the four circles (2-5) which in descending order succeed the first. Sins from corrupt will are punished in the four lower circles (6-9), or city of Dis.

This main division of the wicked into two classes is taken from the Ethics of Aristotle, as Dante himself (Cantos VI. and XI.) fully **expounds**. Dante is very precise, like a professional engineer, in describing these circles and their subdivisions.

The **occupants of** the first circle are unpunished; they sigh, **because eternally** excluded **from heaven.** The frivolous are merely stung, outwardly **by insects and from within** by their **own aimless** propensities. But yet they are in Hell. Thus, **not pain but** hopelessness is the distinctive attribute common **to every dweller in the** Inferno, just as repentance marks **the** Purgatorio, and spiritual communion the Paradiso.

This hopelessness is characteristically and not unnecessarily **indicated three** times in the third canto. First, **by the dismal inscription** above the gate of Hell, applicable to whomsoever it **contains.** Next (as quoted by Carlyle), when the case of the **frivolous is told by** Virgil. Lastly, Charon says to the sinners, **before he ferries** them across the dark river, 'Hope not ever to **see heaven.'**

Dante puts forth his gravest powers in this inimitably **picturesque canto, the only** one wherein all the inhabitants of **the Inferno are presented.** Coleridge has noted its 'wonderful **profoundness.'** The **severe side** of the poet is most effectually **displayed when he** depicts the state of the frivolous, of those **whose character is** thoroughly unlike his own. Their place is **never named.** Not **a word of** articulate speech, but **cries merely,** do we get from them. Particular mention is made of **one only, and this** is done by **way of** periphrasis. Dante **himself scarcely** speaks of them. He dismisses them with extreme contempt as 'the set of caitiffs hateful to God and to **his enemies;** these scoundrels **who never were alive.'** With **fine observation** he notices their pauseless pursuit **of a flag;** for **such spurious energy, by** a strange contradiction, is often shown **by swarmers (we may see it** daily **in our** streets with restless pleasure-seekers; **we may** read it on the features of giddy **nursemaids,** whirling along perambulators containing children **for whom they** care nothing). It is Virgil who explains to **Dante their** wretched condition—'This miserable mode those **sad souls** maintain who lived without infamy and without **praise.** Mingled are they with **that** caitiff choir of angels who were not rebellious nor **were** faithful unto God but were **for themselves.** Heaven chases them out, not to be less fair. **Nor** does deep Hell receive them, lest the wicked should **have from them any glory.'** Dante then asks—'Master, what grieves them so much, that **they lament thus loudly?'** Virgil answers —' **I will tell it thee** very **briefly. These** have no hope of **death, and** their blind life is so **low** that they are envious of **every** other lot. **Fame of** them the world does **not allow to exist.** Mercy and justice disdain them. **Let us not speak of** them, but look and pass.'

This last sentence (Carlyle's second quotation) **is one of** those few passages in which our English gives, without loss of style, the full meaning of the original; the monosyllabic words reminding us of some of Shakespeare's most emphatic lines, best suited to solemn topics, like the—' Aye, but to **die and go** we know not where' of *Measure for Measure.*

When the pious and gentle Abbé de Saint-Cyran, shortly **before** his death, wrote, 'que les foibles sont plus à craindre **quelquefois que les méchants,'** he drew a faint **but exact parallel to one side of the powerful** Dante. (*Port-Royal,* par Sainte-Beuve, Livre 2, xiii.)

Page 93.—*Purgatorio.*—Carlyle **has elsewhere** reiterated his preference for the Purgatorio. **But he goes too far** in attributing the greater attention commonly paid the Inferno ' to our general Byronism of taste.' The Inferno comes first and must be read first; otherwise the Divine Comedy is not intelligible. Simply through laziness or want of leisure many fail to pursue their studies beyond ' the first song, which is about the sunken.' (Inferno, XX., 3.)

Page 95.—*Paradiso.*—The Paradiso **is more difficult than** the **two other** songs, not in style but in subject-matter, which by its nature **remains** ætherial, intangible, unearthly. For both Hell and Purgatory belong to our globe and Dante himself has said in a letter—' I **found** the original of my Hell in the **world** which we inhabit.' (See Isaac D'Israeli's paper on ' The **Origin of Dante's Inferno.'**) Yet has the Paradiso never quite **wanted some devoted English appreciators.** Thus we read of young Hallam, the hero of *In Memoriam*—'Like all genuine worshippers of the great Florentine Poet, he rated the Inferno below the two later portions of the *Divina Comedia;* there was nothing even to revolt his taste, but rather much to attract it, in the scholastic theology and mystic visions of the Paradiso.'

The Paradiso is so beautiful throughout that quotations from it lose much by their removal from the context, a sure sign of perfect works of art (as with Mozart's operas, compared to those of other composers). We may refer, however, to one passage at the opening of Canto XXVII. When Dante hears all Paradise beginning to chant their hymn of glory to the Trinity, he says—'that the sweet song intoxicated me. What I saw seemed to me the smile of the universe.' He had previously used the same concept of inebriation to indicate the very opposite extreme of feeling in the first lines of Canto XXIX. of the Inferno, which Coleridge cites as a chosen specimen of 'the endless subtle beauties of Dante.' We are here, curiously enough, reminded of Byron—

'Man, being reasonable, must get drunk;
The best of life is but intoxication.'

The reader should study the instructive 'parallel between Dante and Petrarch' to be found in the *Essays* of Ugo Foscolo.

LECTURE VI.

Page 98.—*Galileo*.—It is insufficiently known that Galilei was not only great as a man of science; he is also among the most charming of writers. His dialogues sparkle with the liveliest humour. Asked why he wrote so well, he said he was fond of reading Ariosto.

Galilei did more than Luther for the cause of real belief, by freeing men's minds from subjection to the tyranny of ecclesiastical opinions. Luther and his successors but endeavoured to substitute one kind of priestly domination for another. Galilei taught serious enquirers how they should begin if they sincerely wished to study nature for themselves. Let the way be cleared by getting rid of prevailing errors, that we may see in what direction the truth lies, and then methodically pursue it. The

Copernican point of view was not a thing fixed before Galilei entered on his labours. He it was who effectually subverted previous confusing notions; who showed the remoteness and littleness **of man, no longer** occupying **the centre of all** things, though **capable of** becoming great by the pious exercise of **those powers which reveal** to him his true relations to the **universe.**

The clergy, from their point of view, beheld the wide firmament (that is to say, almost everything which exists) **as** a ceiling stretched above man's unshining abode. **To** this restricted opinion they had adjusted their dogmas; and these, in the course of time, were threatened with the fate of the worn-out geocentric hypothesis. It is often now said that we are irreligious because we have abandoned our faith in miracles. Not so, but men ask what provision has been made to save the souls who are on the planet Jupiter? The Church, therefore, was right in persecuting Galilei.

'The moral law, in its application to man, is not the same, **if (1) the** earth *revolves* or if (2) she is *motionless* in space. Were she motionless, man evidently would have the right **to believe himself** the principal object of the Creator's thoughts; **but she revolves,** and henceforth man is **no more** than the **privileged** being **of** one of **the millions of worlds** circulating **within** infinite space. That **is very** different; and this it is **which** has **been** perfectly comprehended by the *very pious folks* **of a** certain **epoch.** Those who condemned Galileo, Copernicus, Giordano Bruno . . . were logical in their ignorance : 'tis this which excuses them. Piety did not suffice to teach us whether the earth revolves or not; that, science alone could do.' (Translated from *Analyse élémentaire de l'Univers,* par G. A. Hirn. Paris, 1868, p. 528.)

Professor Mach, of Prag, has given us the best account of Galilei as the founder of modern dynamics, the worthy precursor of Huyghens and Newton. His book (*Die Mechanik,* Leipzig, 1883) contains a copy of the fine old portrait of 'the Tuscan artist' on whose friendly features our own Milton was permitted to gaze.

Men of science are often absurdly contrasted with men of literature. I feel it good to remember that, thirty years ago,

Mr. Huxley was the first person who kindly explained to me some passages in Dante, the last and the greatest of the geocentrists.

Page 101.—*Printing.*—The date of 1450, assigned in the text to the full utilisation of this invention, is rather too early. Yet 1440 has often been mentioned, as in the Essay prefixed to the edition of Pascal's *Provincial Letters* published by the elder Didot.

Discussions as to the origin of printing have a more than antiquarian interest, although much of the evidence for their exact treatment seems wanting. We can hardly deny that Gutenberg was the real inventor of printing. Poverty and his necessary dependence on extraneous artistic aid threw him into the hands of Fust and Schoeffer, who from Gutenberg's workshop issued at Mayence in 1454 copies of the famous letters of indulgence, the first sheet printed from moveable types which we are now able to verify. At the close of 1455 or beginning of 1456 the same pair published the first printed book, the so-called Mazarin Bible, which Gutenberg years before had begun. A year later followed their Psalter of 1457, the first printed book bearing a date. Gutenberg, turned out of his laboratory, set up another, and in 1460 issued the *Catholicon* of Balbi. The merit of executing this work has also been snatched from Gutenberg by some of his pupils and others. The slowness and secrecy with which he had to labour not only injured poor Gutenberg in his life-time, but have since tended to hurt his reputation.

That printing came late, that it was not devised at a stroke, that its inventor long toiled amid darkness and difficulties which have obscured his nobleness, his self-abnegation, his identity; further, that its products were soon spread abroad, and that, unlike other arts, it reached rapidly a high state of relative perfection—need not now surprise us. These things are at once explained if we bear in mind the many disciplines, antecedent and collateral, which this invention demands, and consider the wonderful results it is fitted to effect with peoples ready to receive its influence.

R

Page 102.—*Gunpowder.*—The results of the invention of gunpowder, dispassionately regarded as the typical species of the **genus** explosive, the *editio princeps* of a classical gospel preached to moderns (harmonising and conflicting, in the most intricate manner, with the teachings of other uncontroverted gospels, which appeal likewise to the passions of fear, greed, or vanity) may be viewed as they affect (*a*) professional fighters and (*b*) students of history.

(*a*) Napoleon, a brilliant operator because he was a deep thinker in the art of war, is here our highest authority. He expresses clearly his opinion that certain qualities must have been common to the great generals of all times, and that they owed their advantages to the exercise of these rather than to fortune. But he says further that, supposing the Elysian fields should send back to earth the choicest of the dead, less than a day's notice would enable Gustavus Adolphus or Turenne to fight efficiently a modern battle, while Alexander, Cæsar, or Hannibal would need at least one or two months to study what can be done with gunpowder ('Notes sur l'histoire de la Guerre,' in *Correspondance*, **Tome** XXXI., p. 501).

(*b*) The historian, as well as the military man, will reflect that the effects of gunpowder are twofold—physical and moral. It kills men at a distance, in great numbers at once, often with little skill, sometimes without danger to the aggressor, and usually by means which readily permit repeated application. It awes men because it may be used by unseen foes, because its action is swift and may find them unprepared, and because skill can do little or nothing to thwart it.

Hence the fear of death or wounds thus produced, the attendant uncertainty and such circumstances, immediately influencing the senses, as noise or smoke overcomes enemies rendered careful of lives which in hand-to-hand encounters they would freely venture.

Gunpowder is merciful because by it (1) battles are soon decided and (2) victory cannot long be concealed. With cold steel it is imperative that a small disciplined army slaughter a considerable proportion of those opposed to them. Read, for example, the account in Gibbon (*Decline*, Chap. XIX.) of the battle of Strasburg, fought A.D. 357 by the Emperor Julian aga.nst the fierce barbarian Chnodomar. It must often have been difficult for ancient conquerors to know when they had won. We should therefore dismiss many charges of cruelty brought against Cæsar and other illustrious captains of antiquity.

Improvements of explosive weapons enhance their merciful tendencies. On the Franco-Prussian warfields in 1870, with needle-guns and chassepots, fewer proportionally were shot than with the flint-muskets fired at the battle of Albuera in 1811. In this terrible engagement seventy per cent. of the victors were placed *hors de combat* (Napier's *Peninsular War*, Book XII., Chap. VI.).

It is true that non-explosive like explosive weapons act both on men's minds and bodies. But the former exert less influence morally, notwithstanding that, with strict irony, they are more sure in their physical operation.

The spear and the sword suggest feudal times and privileged persons. Gunpowder is a leveller, the fit precursor of our democracy. The weakest can use it, the strongest suffer from it. Its action, like that of fate, appears accidental; premeditated as to its causes, its incidence is mechanical. Thus it is doubly dreaded. It is less horrible to be killed by a man than by a machine.

> 'It has a strange quick jar upon the ear,
>   That cocking of a pistol, when you know
> A moment more will bring the sight to bear
>   Upon your person, twelve yards off, or so.'

Hotspur's popinjay was rightly frightened at 'vile guns.' As the improvement of lethal weapons progresses, so does the unwillingness of men to be hit by them increase in a more than corresponding ratio (see 'The Warfare of the Future' by A. Forbes, *Nineteenth Century*, May 1891). Perhaps in times to come every bullet will not have its billet.

Page 104.—*The Spanish Nation.*—Prescott's *Ferdinand and Isabella* is more instructive and appreciative than any other book we can cite on the leading facts in the history of Spain and the distinguished qualities of its once eminent people.

Nor is Prescott despondent as to the future which may yet be in store for the Spaniards.

Page 107.—*Mahomet.*—Carlyle refers to Mohammed from the same point of view in his *Lectures on Heroes.* Space fails us for the discussion of this tempting and very interesting topic. The reader is referred to Gibbon's treatment of it (see Chap. L. of his *Decline*, with the copious notes of Dr. W. Smith's edition) and to the learned Wellhausen's article on Mohammed (in the ninth edition of the *Ency. Britannica*).

That Mohammed was either a true prophet or an impostor (a deceiver of himself and others from first to last) states two contradictory opinions which in words are very easily expressed, but neither of which considerate students can accept as satisfactory. The first of these opinions receives some support from facts; the second must be rejected, in spite of much plausible criticism. Neither Jews, professing Christians nor infidels are likely to be fair judges of Mohammed as he really was, unless their minds are capable, in an extraordinary degree, of standing aside from the prejudices of education. The intermediate hypotheses—that Mohammed began in sincerity and ended in deception, or that his whole life shows a mixture of faith and scepticism, are somewhat more tenable. But they are also more ambiguous and less conclusive. Rather did Mohammed waver, not between belief and doubt, but between belief as modified by contemplation or by practice. Like all distinguished men he displays a union, intricate enough, of weakness and strength. Powerfully as he moulded many circumstances by his will, their force sometimes compelled him to say things in apparent opposition to what he thought and did. Moses, too, was impeded in his good intentions by external necessities, affecting men's minds, opportunities and acquired habits. We do not sufficiently allow for the extreme sensitiveness inherent in several great men of action, such as Cæsar, Mohammed and Napoleon. They may disguise this by their power of rapid reflection, enabling them to utilise what seem to others defects, to derive fresh energy from the high tension of their repressed sufferings. Archbishop Whately (*Lessons on Mind*, p. 174) indicates 'a sort of intermediate state of mind

between belief and disbelief.' He illustrates his subject by
reference to Cowper's poem — 'The Castaway.' This weak
though **amiable** and gifted **man** offers the strongest possible
contrast to Mohammed; but such remote analogies are, in one
essential particular, often the truest of all. It can scarcely be
said with truth that conviction implies the initial absence of
doubt, the power to question the crude assumptions others
would impose on **us**. The exemplary hero of *In Memoriam*
gathered strength and gained a stronger faith by fighting his
doubts, not by ignoring them; but dogmatic theologians do not
commend Hallam's method. The progress of Mohammedanism
after the death of its founder; its persistence and extension to
this day, notwithstanding hostile **missionaries, politicians** and
armies; its suitability to many and diverse peoples — **these**
things declare, better than historical comments, how vast was
the plan this man set himself to devise, how exceptional were
the endowments by which he achieved it.

It is well known that Goethe's mind was long occupied by
reflections on Mohammed, whom he once intended to make the
hero of **a drama** (see his *Life* by Lewes, Book III., Chap. 4).
He has left us as a fragment *Mahomet's Gesang*. He himself
translated the **Mahomet** of Voltaire, played at the Weimar
theatre in 1800.

Heinrich Heine's account (*Englische Fragmente*, XII.) **of his**
visit to **the** London docks shows how genial is the response an
appeal to the prophet's name can evoke from believers.

Page 112.—*Humour of Cervantes.*—In this quality (good
judges now admit) Cervantes is surpassed by no writer. The
scene of Don Quixote's visor immortalises a recurrent weakness
of all reformers.

Don Quixote, Robinson Crusoe, and *Gulliver's Travels* are
unquestionably the masterpieces of fiction. Perhaps the *Vicar
of Wakefield* and *Tom Jones* should be added to the list. England, relatively weak in the fields of history and the drama
(Shakespeare, a mighty exception, deducted), shines well in this
comparison, which attests the glowing imagination and rich
descriptive gifts of its best literary representatives. Still *Don
Quixote* remains the freshest **of** novels, if by **a** name since

applied to so many worthless productions, it may be now thus designated.

Page 113.—*Lope and Calderon.*—A little volume—*The Spanish Drama*, 1846, by the late G. H. Lewes, is almost wholly devoted to a very readable account of these skilful and prolific play-writers.

Page 114.—*Spanish Literature.*—For a good guide to the authors Carlyle does not notice see the English translation of Bouterwek's *History of Spanish and Portuguese Literature*, in two vols. 1823.

LECTURE VII.

Page 118.—*Pytheas.*—The scanty fragments left us from the lost writings of this traveller (whom Strabo, when he cites him, loves to contradict) are little known. But see the 'Eclaircissemens sur la vie et les voyages de Pythéas de Marseille,' par M. De Bougainville, in Tome XIX. of the *Mémoires de l'Académie royale des Inscriptions et Belles-Lettres.*

Page 122.—*William Tell.*—A chapter under this title, showing how the story about shooting the apple arose, may be read in *Curious Myths of the Middle Ages*, by S. Baring-Gould.

Page 123.—*Comines.*—Scott drew largely upon this writer in the preparation of two of his romances, *Quentin Durward* and *Anne of Geierstein*. The historian appears as an acting personage in the first of these works.

Page 127.—*Luther found a Bible.*—His doing so, an event nowise extraordinary, has in our time been made a subject for much misrepresentation by Protestants of the untruthful aggressive sort. In *The Dark Ages*, by the Rev. S. R. Maitland (a valuable book, lately reprinted) will be found a clear account of the matter.

Page 131.—*Ulphilas.*—The significance of the work done by this estimable and much-abused bishop is well explained in Max Müller's *Science of Language.*

Page 131.—*Luther's words half battles.*—Jean Paul was anticipated as to his motive for this comparison. Quintilian says of Cæsar, that he seemed to speak as he had fought.

Page 132.—*Erasmus.*—Bayle's articles on Erasmus, Hutten and Luther abound in fair and instructive comments on many things touching these reformers. What Bayle says or suggests, in his very pleasant manner, has been often in substance pilfered and clumsily refitted to suit the views of those who care more for their own narrow views than for truth and honesty.

Page 136.—*Epistolæ Obscurorum Virorum.*—A full paper on these letters, with much concerning von Hutten, will be found in Sir W. Hamilton's *Discussions.*

LECTURE VIII.

Page 141.—*Mascov.*—Geschichte der Deutschen bis zum Abgang der Meroving. Könige, Leipzig, 1726–37. In 2 vols. 4to. 'The first German historian [says Ebert] who undertook to write the history of the *nation* (not merely of the *empire*).' Translated into English, 1737–38.

Page 142.—*Saxons.*—Consult about this people Klemm's *Germanische Alterthumskunde*, Dresden, 1836, and the word *Saxa* in the *Glossarium* of Du Cange.

As to Saxon being to this day the Celtic name for the English—read in the *Life and Letters of Rowland Williams D.D.* (Vol. I., p. 179) how this excellent clergyman introduced his wife to his parishioners, ' and when, as in duty bound, they made some complimentary speech (of course in Welsh), his reply in the same language was, "Ah, she is only a poor creature; she can only speak Saesneg!"'

Page 145.—*Normans and English.*—The spoken English language shows in its *grammar* convincing traces of its Teutonic origin, although, in consequence of the Norman conquest and other influences, the number of Norman (or rather Græco-Latin) *words* our dictionaries contain is double that from all other sources. We call English a mixed language with much confusion of thought, best dispelled by studying that serviceable book—Max Müller's *Science of Language*.

Page 146.—*Elizabeth.*—If England, as Carlyle states, was first consolidated under Queen Elizabeth's grandfather, so had France gained the blessings of peace, post-offices, strength and union when guided by a far greater ruler, Louis XI., who died two years before Henry VII. came to the throne. In that same ominous year (1483) of the French king's death were born, by a strange conjuncture, the pious artist Raphael and Luther, the potent disturber of nations. Europe was not long permitted to enjoy quiet. Yet England, as well as France, began at once to progress as soon as the former, after the wars of the Roses, ceased interfering with the affairs of the latter. When the English, under the younger Pitt, resumed their meddling policy, in support of the wretched Bourbons whom they could not keep on their thrones, much misery for both peoples was again brought about. And we are still galled by the weight of debt and taxes then imposed on us.

Page 147.—*Shakespeare.*—The essential resemblance of Shakespeare to Homer, in spite of obvious distinctions, is not the vain thing spurious criticism would make it. Both combine ease and strength, subtlety and naïveté of expression, in a mode only possible to artists of the highest genius.

That Shakespeare indulged in *conceits* of language, after the manner of the Spanish and Italian dramatists, is undeniable. But so did the severe Dante. Playfulness in the handling of words pleases expectant hearers, reveals while it conceals the greater skill of the master, relieves his tension of mind, not unbecomingly places him on a level with his audience, and above all is necessary to the contrasted effect of those serious passages he must introduce.

Page 148.—*Poet and* **Thinker**.—No considerate person opposes the poet to the thinker, for thought involves sentiment and will as well as purely intellectual processes. (See Wundt, *System der Philosophie*, Leipzig, 1889, p. 41).

Coleridge (*Notes* **and** *Lectures upon Shakespeare*, p. 6) says—'Poetry is not **the** proper **antithesis** to prose, but **to** science. Poetry is opposed to science, and prose to metre.' But is it not more correct to distinguish science, strictly so called, from art in general? And is there not a still more real distinction between conscious logical operations of the mind and those imaginative gifts by which both the poet and the man of science may profit?

Page 151.—*The greatest* **men quiet.**—The finest proof of this truth is afforded by **one of the greatest of all writers,** Cæsar, to those who are capable of reading him **between the lines. The brief gentle** references of this powerful man of action to the blunders of his subordinates, **the quiet** way in **which he passes over his** own exploits, his manner of speaking (or rather, not speaking) **of** himself are at once delightful and awful. No so-called religious leader has ever gained victories **over others and** himself like those of **this** immortal pagan conqueror. I could name two men of genuine **ability,** both of humble origin, unprejudiced and unspoilt **by books,** who felt **almost** inclined to worship Cæsar's bust in the British Museum. The age of heroism is not dead, so long as this is possible. Read what the late Richard Jefferies says of Cæsar's lineaments in *The Story of my Heart.*

Page 152.—*John Knox.*—The character of Knox will scarcely be upheld by Carlyle's eulogies. We may willingly recognise his unusual courage; such men are rare, and he who is not a coward fairly claims our praise. But Catiline also was a very courageous man. Hume's *History* tells us how Knox successively **persecuted two** queens, Mary of England and Mary Queen of Scots. As an indication of his unrivalled coarseness of language read 'The first blast of the trumpet against the monstrous regiment of women.' To learn his powers of tergiversation (for Knox, with his scholastic training, could play the logician's part, denounced in others by Carlyle as antagonistic to sincere belief) consider how he afterwards behaved when Queen Elizabeth came to the throne. Maury (*Essai sur les Légendes Pieuses du Moyen-age*) indeed says that Knox 'était un halluciné.' See his article in Bayle and what is told of him by the Rev. S. R. Maitland, in his *Essays on the Reformation.*

Page 159.—*Milton.*—Milton loved what was good in the Puritans, but he who sung of dim religious light and of St. Peter shaking his mitred locks could not be a Puritan at heart. Or rather, the pious author of Adam's evening prayer (*Paradise Lost*, IV., 720-735), than which David, Isaiah and other prophets of old have not left us more inspired utterances, was the only true Puritan of his time, compared to whom nominal Puritans are but as stubble. Milton, like Schiller, was a real lover of liberty, without being an anarchist. In this respect he was superior to Carlyle, who shows himself an oligarch whenever he deliberately states his political opinions and is full of that *morgue aristocratique* which Napoleon declared to be, next to money-making, the highest creed of Englishmen, of middle-class Englishmen most of all. The American descendants of the Puritans still, in secret, cultivate this weed. The French, the Swiss and the Dutch are comparatively free from it. So long as Germany cherishes it, its unity will be spurious; with all its strength and discipline, it will have this disadvantage, should it fight its internally unfettered antagonist. Strange irony of fate—that the least and the most despotic of the great European powers, the first liberators and the last persecutors of the Jews, should now be united against that nation in which feudalism maintains an influence out of concert with the enlightenment and strong character of its hitherto unconquered inhabitants.

LECTURE IX.

Mr. Anstey was hindered by an attack of malaria from attending Carlyle's ninth lecture. The reader, while regretting the absence of his reporter, will console himself with the rellection that this lecture has been lost rather than any of the others. What the Lecturer had to say on French literature may well be conjectured from the long papers on Diderot and Voltaire, reprinted in his *Miscellanies.*

Strongly sympathising, as did Carlyle, with certain aspects of the French Revolution, and powerfully as he has represented several of its scenes, he never could rightly appreciate French views of things. We regret here to find him in good company; for Coleridge, De Quincey, and many worthy English authors exhibit a like deficiency.

LECTURE X.

Page 161.—*Quotation from Goethe.*—But Goethe also said, 'My inheritance, how wide, how fair! Time is my estate; to Time I'm heir.'

Page 163.—*Reign of Quackery.*—Carlyle might have added that nowhere is the doctrine that money will buy money's worth more practised than in the land of the almighty dollar, the free country of the free children of his favourite Puritans, who sought (as a female poet, with impious humour, has sung) 'freedom to worship God,' that is, to split into as many denominations as they pleased. See, *inter alia,* Dickens' *American Notes.* This multiplicity of sects, Archdeacon Farrar tells us, is to be taken as a sure sign of sincerity. A more successful preacher of the modern gospel of Mammon, Mr. Jay Gould, improves its text by inserting a trifling marginal gloss; for money now buys what is *not* money's worth. He means 'L'argent des autres,' to quote Gaboriau. For has not Mr. Gould honestly declared that without outsiders (the great host of worshippers who, with innocent and touching credulity, like all true believers, kiss the rod and rejoice when they are robbed) speculators on the Stock Exchange, the high priests of the temple in Wall Street, would certainly starve? The demon of credit (called by Addison a goddess!), sitting on his stool in the infernal counting-house, must view with an evil eye these ready-money transactions.

Carlyle's second doctrine (taken from Byron), that Pleasure

is pleasant, holds true, but chiefly for beginners and fresh converts. It is milk for babes. Happily, pleasure soon palls upon those who get more than their share of it, and thus the distribution less of pleasure than of pain is more equable in our life than the ignorant suppose. Philippe de Comines, commenting on the King's death, says—'Poor and mean folks ought to have little hope about this world, since so great a king suffered and toiled so much, and could not find one hour to push off his death, whatever diligence he knew to make' (*Memoires*, VI., Chap. XIII). And again he writes (*Ibid.* VIII., Chap. XIII. Note the ominous number of the chapter in both books)—'No creature is exempt from suffering, and all eat their bread in pain and grief. Our Lord promised it when he made mankind and has loyally kept it with all people. But pains and griefs are different; those of the body are the least, and those of the understanding the greatest; those of the wise are of one sort, those of fools of another. Yet too much grief and suffering afflicts the fool like the sage (though to many it seems the contrary), and he has less consolation. Poor people (who toil and plough, to feed themselves and their children, and pay taxes and subsidies to their lords) ought to live in great discomfort, if great princes and lords had all the world's pleasures, and they toil and misery; but things go on quite otherwise.'

Page 165.—*Speech and Silence.*—The saying quoted by Carlyle is an old oriental one, though it has had many modern editions. Thus Schleiermacher says, in praise of a great scholar—'Bekker is silent in seven languages.'

Page 167.—*Whitfield.*—A favourable view of Whitfield is taken by Lord Mahon (Stanhope) in Chapter XIX. of his *History of England*.

Page 168.—*Steele.*—Thackeray has, perhaps better than any other writer, said a good word for the neglected Steele, whose fine panegyric on one woman well rivals the more famous quotations made from Petrarch or Dante on like subjects. We love Steele; we praise, but seldom read Addison.

Page 169.—*Swift.*—Carlyle refers here to the lines in Johnson's *Vanity of Human Wishes*—

'From Marlborough's eyes the tears of dotage flow,
And Swift expires a driveller and a show.'

It is cruel to quote them. The beauty and strength of Swift's unsurpassed prose are the product of a clear intellect and a genuine (if not always apparent) fineness of feeling, rarely found united in Englishmen. Swift is too honest not to show us his faults; we therefore the more willingly pardon them. *A Tale of a Tub* demands his canonisation by Anglicans, could they see how true and badly treated a friend they had in him. His *Gulliver's Travels*, the charmer of our childhood, the instructor and amuser of our later years, is simply (we speak advisedly) the best work of pure imagination ever put forth, after the *Divine Comedy* of Dante. The genius of Bunyan, in spite of his high theme, does not so impress us, with all his allegorical names and characters. But in reading Swift and Dante their perfect style is forgotten, because it is perfect; we think only of the real things they describe and the characters who act again in our presence. We are not told that Capaneus rag*es*; we hear him rag*ing*. We become Lilliputians ourselves when the Emperor of Lilliput appears. 'He is taller, by almost the breadth of my nail, than any of his court, which alone is enough to strike an awe into the beholders.' Great is the power of words, in themselves the idlest things, when used by a master.

Page 170.—*Sterne.*—Sterne (like Rabelais, whom in many respects he resembles less than critics pretend) is, in one word, indescribable. He should be read, not criticised. He has certainly some of the merits of Cervantes and Swift; his humour is as exquisite, but very different and all his own. Coleridge, strange to say, has best commented on him (a Course of Lectures, IX., in Vol. II. of his *Notes*). Dr. Slop, Corporal Trim, the Widow Wadman and Uncle Toby are quite as real to us as Don Quixote himself. The improprieties of Sterne are indeed provoking, but we pity those who see not the refinement which lies beside them. In subtlety of conception and expression the character of Mr. Shandy is worthy of Shakespeare.

We praise many books more; but there are few we would not part with for a comfortable fireside copy of the inimitable *Tristram Shandy*.

Page 171.—*Pope*.—An affected contempt for Pope, whom they do not understand, is one of the symptoms common to a sickly class of modern essayists, who spin weak cobwebs about him from their own ailing moral interior. Byron knew better when he called Pope 'a poet of a thousand years.' He is not to be spoken of in the same breath with the other poets of Queen Anne's contemptible reign. His *Essay on Criticism* remains a marvellous performance, though written in his twentieth year. Notwithstanding Hallam's pseudo-platonic criticism (*Literature of Europe*, Chap. I.) *Eloisa to Abelard* most touchingly expresses the feelings of one of the truest of women, while the immortal *Dunciad* asks in vain for a twin-brother, to stigmatise the obtrusive pretenders to fame swarming in our nineteenth century.

Page 173.—*Johnson and Boswell*.—The reader should again compare Carlyle's essay on Johnson with that of Macaulay, and note well the superiority of the former.

The recent edition of *Boswell* by Dr. Hill treats this masterpiece of biography with unusual care and sympathy.

Page 174.—*Hume*.—Hume (against all differences of opinion) ranks with Malebranche in France and Leibniz in Germany as one of the few modern writers who, like Plato and Cicero among the ancients, knew how to make philosophy agreeable. See the edition of his works in four vols., by Green and Grose.

Page 176.—*Robertson*.—Robertson is the baby Carlyle flings to the wolves, that he may save the reputation of other Scotchmen whom he always pets. Even our James I. (his James VI.) won his admiration.

Page 177.—*Gibbon*.—Gibbon, the only Englishman who has united German learning with French grace, is less understood by Carlyle than by many of the orthodox, admirers of the finely tempered weapon that wounds them. Carlyle used more moderate language in talking to Emerson. 'Gibbon he called the splendid bridge from the old world to the new.' He is still the only general historian for the whole period of the Middle Ages. Unfortunately the latest and best annotated edition of his *Decline* has penuriously been printed on very poor paper.

LECTURE XI.

Page 179.—*Inadequacy of Logic.*—What Carlyle here states resembles, more closely perhaps than he might have wished, the opinions set forth on the same subject by Cardinal Newman, with all his characteristic charm of expression (see *An Essay in Aid of the Grammar of Assent*).

Page 185.—*Werter and Charlotte on Tea-cups.*—In the poem expressive of gratitude to his kind friend and patron the Duke of Weimar, among his Roman elegies, Goethe thus wrote—

'Yet what avails it me, that indeed the Chinese, too,
   Painted, with careful hand, Werter and Lotte on glass.'

This translation is literal. But see the whole poem, with much else that is enjoyable, in Mrs. Austin's *Characteristics of Goethe*, 3 vols., London, 1833.

Page 187.—*The Works of Byron.*—Byron never seriously said that the world was a place not worthy for generous men to live in. He says quite the contrary. Upbraiding the degenerate inhabitants of the beautiful land of Greece, before it regained its freedom, he refers to the time 'when man was worthy of thy clime.' In the same poem (see the delicious verses at the beginning of *The Giaour*) he often expresses the same sentiment. For example—

'Strange—that where Nature loved to trace,
As if for Gods, a dwelling-place,
And every charm and grace hath mix'd
Within the paradise she fix'd,
There man, enamour'd of distress,
Should mar it into wilderness.'

And again—
> 'So soft the scene, so form'd for joy,
> So curst the tyrants that destroy.'

The burning stanzas of his inspiriting *Isles of Greece* exquisitely display the same conviction.

Page 188.— *Goetz von Berlichingen*.— Sir Walter Scott translated, not well, this poem, in which the characters are thoroughly alive, and which Goethe wrote as a young man beginning to show his strength, and anxious for a while to save his mind from the oppression caused by the symptoms of weakness he saw around him. Goetz is the pendant to Werter. It expresses the mediæval spirit, as against the modern. Goetz struggles to the last; Werter is worn out. The truth is that Goethe, writing these poems out of his heart, in quick succession, split his own complex being into two characters, the man of contemplation and the man of action. In *Faust* this double theme is again taken up on a much greater scale, both as to extent and intricacy, and with far more refined mental resources.

Those who neglect *Werter's Leiden*, fearing it should prove too melancholy, are deceived. It contains not a few bright thoughts and many charming descriptions of external nature.

Page 191.— *The Diamond Necklace*.— The reader will, doubtless, turn to Carlyle's paper on this matter (reprinted in his *Miscellanies*), and to the well-known romance of Alexandre Dumas (*Le collier de la reine*). The English 'Baccarat scandal' of 1891 might, like the affair of the Diamond Necklace (which it more resembles than at first appears), have caused mischief, had attendant circumstances aided. It, too, was a spark, which by good luck did not fall upon gunpowder.

Page 192.—*Rousseau*.—For an instructive and very pleasantly written lecture on Rousseau, which many of our readers have probably not seen, we cite the title of Emil Du Bois-Reymond's 'Friedrich II. und Jean-Jacques Rousseau,' in his *Reden*, erste Folge, Leipzig, 1886.

As Rousseau, like Don Quixote (see the English translation

of Griesinger's *Mental Diseases*, p. 10), with all his exquisite genius, reminds us of those who belong to the so-called borderland between sanity and insanity, we may refer also to *J.-J. Rousseau's Kranheitsgeschichte* von P. J. Möbius, Leipzig, 1889. See, likewise, the somewhat rare *Exposé succinct* de la contestation qui s'est élevée entre M. Hume et M. Rousseau, avec les pièces justificatives (à Londres, 1766) and Mr. John Morley's welcome *Life* of this eminent French writer. Diseased nerves, in spite of Carlyle's protest, sometimes offer the only true explanation of the strange conduct of great men.

Page 193.—*The French Revolution.*—For a calm and hopeful discussion, written with much eloquence, of the ideas suggested by a study of the three French revolutions (1789-1830-1848) every reader should think over Ernest Renan's *L'Avenir de la Science: Pensées de* 1848. Paris, 1890.

Page 194.—*Europe and France.*—Carlyle is not consistent in asserting the right of Europe against France, while he commends Napoleon's maxim of 'the career open to talents.' The English and the Germans threatened France in the first instance, and caused a misery more widespread than that of the French Revolution itself, by their vicious intromission in the affairs of a people with which they had no concern. The two Teutonic nations, in fact if not in right, were consistent enough. Whatever they might say, they showed by their actions they preferred to freedom that slavery to oligarchical governments it was the chief business of the French Revolution to put down. These things began before Buonaparte. It is wrong to look on him as an upsetter of the principles of the Revolution. He indeed saved France from anarchy, restored religion, and raised that nation to a height of power it never reached before or since. But was he not a promulgator from the cannon's mouth of the great revolutionary maxim Carlyle so much admires? And was it not their terror lest Europe in general should find this maxim too captivating, that made its rulers send their misguided hosts against the preacher of a doctrine which, once taught, meant the destruction of all oligarchy?

s

Napoleon said, that John Bull in the end would do him justice. Has not the chief recorder (Gen. Sir W. Napier) of Wellington's victories emphatically asserted the incomparable superiority of his Corsican opponent? Did not our Queen appear in public leaning on the arm of the nephew of her grandfather's enemy, and has not the son of the same nephew since died in her service?

LECTURE XII.

Page 198.—*Return to Nature.*—This is precisely the advice of the leading interlocutor in Galilei's *Dialogo*, published in 1632 (not 1630 as stated by Whewell, whose account, in his *Inductive Sciences*, of this first of modern philosophers is very far from being the best). Besides Mach's chapter on Galilei, already recommended (under p. 98), see Poggendorff's *Geschichte der Physik*, Leipzig, 1879, pp. 204-245, and Heller's *Geschichte der Physik*, Stuttgart, 1882, I. Band, pp. 343-383. Also, the German translation of part of Galilei's *Discorsi* (1638), forming No. 11 of Ostwald's *Klassiker der exacten Wissenschaften*, Leipzig, 1890. Galilei may be called the Homer, while Newton is the Shakespeare of dynamics. Huyghens (the 'Summus Hugenius' of our Newton, a man not prone to distribute praise) is its Sophocles. The merits of Huyghens are well set forth not only by Mach, but also by Dühring in his very original *Kritische Geschichte der Mechanik*, 3 ed. Leipzig, 1887.

Page 199.—*The Phœnix.*—What Carlyle says of the end or consummation of scepticism will be consoling to many, but it is not the view of theologians and logicians, for whom he never cared. The Rev. Dr. Momerie, who belongs to both these classes (a union somewhat rare), tells us that those who still cling to their early faith 'are every now and then pained, embarrassed, staggered, by the fact that so many of their intellectual superiors consider their faith to be absurd. The spirit of agnosticism is in the air. The reviews are full of it. Popular lecturers are everywhere insisting upon it. We meet it in novels, and even in poetry. At the universities it is the predominant creed among the undergraduates and the younger dons. And, worst of all, we hear it sometimes in drawing-rooms from women's lips—from women, strange to say, who are young and fair, who are, or should be, happy' (*Agnosticism*, 3 ed. revised, 1889). We all wish, like the Phœnix, to rise again from our ashes, but it is not quite so pleasant to be reminded that ashes must again and again be our doom. This series of transvolutions, which Carlyle promises us, savours rather of Indian than Christian belief. In his too emphatic declaration of our ignorance (p. 180), in itself sufficiently real, he goes beyond poor Ophelia (*Hamlet*, Act IV., Scene V.) in her frenzy,—' Lord, we know what we are, but we know not what we may be.'

We would point out the frequent error of using ' sceptic as a synonym for the words ' agnostic ' or ' infidel.' Sceptics are extremely rare. We hardly know of any beside Montaigne, Bayle, Hume (perhaps Gibbon and Mill, father and son), with Fontenelle—all delightful writers. Pascal, that matchless writer, had also his sceptical side. He is finely discriminated by Paul Bourget as the only apologist for orthodoxy who ever understood doubters. Most defenders of Christianity, laudably desiring to slay the errors of their opponents, discharge their missiles at everything except the mark. They fail by not discovering the sources of conviction and its opposites. They hit the ambient air. Archbishop Whately and Cardinal Newman have indicated some of these faults of method, but they themselves in practice have likewise failed. Of living eminent writers we may name as sceptics the fervid Renan and the acute Du Bois-Reymond. Among those lately deceased we might also designate as sceptical, in the best and truest sense, one of the choicest geniuses of our time, a discoverer comparable to Newton, the pious Gustav Theodor Fechner. Carlyle, without knowing it, was himself a sceptic.

Page 203.—*Happiness.*—Carlyle, as so many know, has expressed noble thoughts on the signification of happiness in the most remarkable chapter of his *Sartor Resartus* (Book II., Chap. IX.). His friend, John Stuart Mill, referring to these views, has modified them from his own experience (*Autobiography*, pp. 132–143). His theory, strange as this may sound, is very like the only true and pious one: it is, in fact, a moonlight reflection of it. We may, in our ingratitude, reject the happiness offered to us; but happiness is not to be snatched by our own efforts. It comes to us like genius, beauty (Iliadis, III., 65), or sleep (Psalm cxxvii. 2). It is a gift from on high.

Page 204.—*German Metaphysicians.*—We fully admit the inherent difficulties of metaphysics, and the further difficulties superinduced by many painstaking German writers and others; but Carlyle's views of both defy our powers of annotation. They are more incomprehensible than metaphysics themselves.

The best modern works on philosophy are unquestionably the very original and critical writings of Wundt, namely, his *Psychologie, Logik, Ethik, System der Philosophie,* and *Studien,* which last is a most useful periodical by himself and others on all topics appertaining to things of the mind. These books we have bought and read (let others do likewise). They could not, their dates being considered, have come within Carlyle's cognisance. A little more patience in dealing with such subjects would have done our Lecturer no harm. Metaphysics were certainly not Carlyle's *forte*, though he has strangely been cited as a promulgator of idealism. He errs in blaming metaphysic for failing to supply that which (like a custom-house) it can never afford.

Page 205.—*Goethe.*—Carlyle has said so much that is good about Goethe, that no one who possesses his works needs the particular references which are here omitted. He is at his best whenever he treats of him. Between Goethe and Englishmen he still remains the one indispensable medium.

Page 207.—*Westöstlicher Divan.*—See Simrock's edition (Heilbronn, 1875) of this incomparable work, with its references to the original eastern sources from which Goethe drew. Also consult an interesting article ('Goethe und Suleika') in Julian Schmidt's *Bilder aus dem geistigen Leben,* Leipzig, 1870.

Page 208.—*Schiller.*—The cheap edition of Carlyle's *Life of Schiller,* published in 1873, has a supplement on Schiller's parents and sisters. This is chiefly made up of translations from the works of Saupe and others. It is well worth reading, and it touchingly depicts (to use Carlyle's words) 'an unconsciously noble scene of Poverty made *richer* than any California.'

Page 211.—*Wilhelm Tell.*—Wilhelm Tell (though prostituted as a school-book) is, next to *Faust*, the noblest tragedy which has appeared since the times of Shakespeare. The third scene of the fourth act, where Tell struggles with his feelings before slaying the tyrant, is unsurpassed for true pathos and rugged strength of expression. Carlyle has given a translation of this scene in his *Life of Schiller*.

Page 212.—*Richter.*—Jean Paul, unlike Goethe and Schiller, has not been fully translated for English readers. Carlyle himself has left us renderings of two of his stories, chosen by him as thoroughly representative. Two other translations are in Bohn's Libraries—*Levana*, a work on education, and the romantic tale entitled *Flower, Fruit, and Thorn Pieces*.

Page 215.—*Leave-taking.*—Carlyle has been often compared, *sotto voce* and expressly, to each of the three German authors he most loved, and whose works he introduced by his useful labours to so many English readers. He has thus in turn been likened to Goethe, Schiller, and Richter. He is furthest from Goethe, whom he most venerated, to whom his obligations were greatest, and with whom, alone of the three, he entered into personal communion. Goethe, with much of Carlyle's conscientiousness and force, possessed in a large measure those very qualities wherein Carlyle was weakest; for who does not allow Goethe's calm, his fairness, his fine appreciation of all that is essential and beautiful in form? He is accordingly by French admirers and by his own countrymen placed far above his great English interpreter, as a man in every way wider and profounder. Certainly he is more harmonious; he was guided by the key-note of artistic forbearance (the μηδὲν ἄγαν of the Greeks—the *ne quid nimis* of their Latin imitators) with a nicety to which Carlyle could never adjust his own compositions. He at no time made any such pretensions. It were useless, therefore, to pursue this comparison further.

Yet surely Carlyle deserves praise for perceiving, as he did, the distinctive excellence of Goethe. This virtue is enhanced when we reflect on the differences between these two writers. To revere what we lack ourselves is the genuine nucleus of piety. We find good in the humblest man when he admires the teacher who shows him a little part of the road to the infinite. There were strong ties of attraction between Carlyle and Goethe. How else could Carlyle have translated so beautifully the charming verses in *Wilhelm Meister?* Through these versions he shines as a true poet, and not a mere satellite, fitted only to reflect the light of the sun of Weimar.

Goethe sincerely esteemed Carlyle's *Life of Schiller*, who is not wholly unlike his biographer. Carlyle surpassed Schiller in the important gift of humour and in dogged industry. In other respects Schiller appears his equal or superior. Both were historians. Carlyle was more copious, more descriptive, more vehement; in quiet strength, in smoothness, in love of liberty, in his firmer and more psychological grasp of the ruling ideas which persist from age to age, the author of *The Thirty-years' War* transcends the sturdy chronicler of the great Frederick, the eloquent but too precipitate commentator on France in her good and evil efforts to obtain freedom. Fine was the dramatic genius of Carlyle, but he diffused what it revealed to him through the general body of his writings. He never so concentrated his powers as to rival those lofty works, worthy of their heroes, *Wilhelm Tell* and *Wallenstein.*

Carlyle comes much closer to Richter, howsoever diverse their gifts and products. To call the latter a writer inferior to Goethe or Schiller is at once true, obvious, unnecessary, meaningless, and invidious. Richter would have shrunk, with real modesty, from the comparison. He has his own excellences; like every noteworthy man of genius he is, in a certain sense, incomparable. The German, like the English Jean Paul (for so is Carlyle often termed), has been well styled the unique, *der einzige*, the only one. Richter resembles Carlyle in his mixture of defects and merits. Both play tricks with language, alternately losing and gaining by risking extraordinary expressions. Both indulge, like St. Paul, in numerous anacolutha. The humour of both is strong, and not always restrained; it highly pleases, it sometimes shocks us. They agree most in the spirit animating their works, their love of innate heroism struggling against outward hindrances, their confidence in the ultimate victory of truth and providence, their hopes for man and their faith in his future. Both were hard workers and high thinkers: none could be more unlike Dante's '*sciaurati che mai non fur vivi.*' Richter and Carlyle were thoroughly instinct with life and with that which is better than life—immortality. That is why they have left such good things behind them. Now they rest from their labours, and their works will follow them. Each might have felt, like Goethe,—

> 'Es kann die Spur von meinen Erdentagen
> Nicht in Aeonen untergehn:'

and have said with Schiller,—

> 'Getröstet können wir zu Grabe steigen:
> Es lebt nach uns;—durch andre Kräfte will
> Das Herrliche der Menschheit sich erhalten,'

THE END.

ELLIS & ELVEY'S PUBLICATIONS.

London: 29 New Bond Street, W.

Two Vols. crown 8vo. cloth gilt, bound from the Author's own design, **18s.**

THE COLLECTED WORKS OF DANTE GABRIEL ROSSETTI.

CONTENTS.

VOL. I. POEMS, PROSE TALES AND LITERARY PAPERS.
VOL. II. TRANSLATIONS (including DANTE'S 'VITA NUOVA' AND THE EARLY ITALIAN POETS), PROSE NOTICES OF FINE ARTS.

Copies can be had in morocco extra, bound from the Author's own design, price **£2 2s.**

Crown 8vo. with Portrait, cloth gilt, price **6s.**

THE POETICAL WORKS OF DANTE GABRIEL ROSSETTI.

EDITED, WITH PREFACE, BY W. M. ROSSETTI.

A NEW EDITION IN ONE VOLUME.

This volume contains all the Original Poems of D. G. Rossetti, as printed in the Collected Works.

The Portrait, which is issued as a Frontispiece, is an engraving by Mr. C. W. SHERBORN, from a Photograph of the Poet taken at Cheyne Walk, Chelsea, in 1864, never before published.

An Edition of 100 Copies was printed upon LARGE PAPER.

Copies can be had in the best Levant morocco, super extra, top edges gilt, (in a variety of styles and colours), price **£1 1s.**

OPINIONS OF THE PRESS.

'A handsome and convenient volume. . . . . Will be valued by many lovers of true poetry.'—*Athenæum.*

'Presented in a very pleasant form.'—*Pall Mall Gazette.*

'The interest of the book is heightened by the excellent portrait of Rossetti, and by the biographical and expository preface furnished by the editor.'—*Globe.*

'Does great credit to its publishers. Mr. W. M. Rossetti's preface calls for nothing but praise.'—*Speaker.*

'This is a volume to be grateful for.'—*Daily Chronicle.*

'Well printed on good paper, and makes a convenient, attractive, and companionable volume.'—*Echo.*

'Neatly bound and well printed, deserves a cordial welcome.'—*Scotsman.*

'In a most convenient and agreeable form . . . . the tasteful volume is sure to find a wide and ready sale.'—*Court Journal.*

'For popular use nothing could be better than this volume.'—*Yorkshire Post.*

'We may well be grateful to Mr. W. M. Rossetti for giving us in this single volume a complete collection of his brother's poems.'—*Yorkshire Herald.*

'All Rossetti's poems are included in the present edition, which, being in one volume, and comparatively cheap, will carry them into wider circles of readers.'—*Glasgow Herald.*

'Messrs. Ellis & Elvey have done considerable service to every lover of fine poetry in issuing a cheap collected edition of Rossetti's poems.'—*Birmingham Weekly Mail.*

'C'est assurément une idée heureuse qu'ont eue les éditeurs Ellis et Elvey d'offrir au public, en un élégant volume, d'un prix accessible, l'ensemble de l'œuvre poétique de Rossetti.'—*Le Livre Moderne.*

ELLIS & ELVEY'S PUBLICATIONS.

D. G. ROSSETTI'S WORKS—continued.

In preparation.

Crown 8vo. cloth gilt, price 6s.

(UNIFORM WITH THE CHEAP EDITION OF ROSSETTI'S POETICAL WORKS.)

DANTE AND HIS CIRCLE:
WITH THE ITALIAN POETS PRECEDING HIM
(1100-1200-1300).
A COLLECTION OF LYRICS
EDITED AND TRANSLATED IN THE ORIGINAL METRES BY
DANTE GABRIEL ROSSETTI.

PART I.
DANTE'S VITA NUOVA, &c.
POETS OF DANTE'S CIRCLE.

PART II.
POETS CHIEFLY BEFORE DANTE.

A NEW EDITION, WITH A NEW PREFACE,
BY W. M. ROSSETTI.

Crown 8vo. cloth gilt, price 6s.

Some French and Spanish Men of Genius.

SKETCHES OF
MARIVAUX, VOLTAIRE, ROUSSEAU, DIDEROT, BEAUMARCHAIS, MIRABEAU, DANTON AND ROBESPIERRE, BERANGER, VICTOR HUGO, EUGENE SUE AND ZOLA, CERVANTES AND LOPE DE VEGA, CALDERON.

BY JOSEPH FORSTER,
AUTHOR OF 'FOUR GREAT TEACHERS,' ETC.

OPINIONS OF THE PRESS.

'Mr. Forster is a sensible and agreeable writer, who is not content with giving his opinion, but who fortifies himself with characteristic extracts from the authors about whom he writes.'—*Daily News.*

'Pleasantly written—interesting and characteristic.'—*Globe.*

'Written in Mr. Forster's agreeable and lucid style, interspersed with well-selected quotations.'—*Gentlewoman.*

'Some agreeable and not unprofitable half-hours may be spent in company with his book.'—*Graphic.*

'A bright little collection of essays. . . . . Mr. Forster, who evidently thinks for himself, has some fresh and ingenious things to say.'—*Star.*

'There pulses through the pages a generous living sympathy with all that is noblest, truest, tenderest, and brightest in humanity, which makes the book very pleasant reading.'—*Court Journal.*

'We appreciate his sketch of Rousseau all the more because that great writer is still too little understood in this country. . . . . Mr. John Morley, who so thoroughly understands Voltaire, fails to understand Rousseau.'—*Echo.*

'It felicitously puts the general reader into possession of a knowledge of the best things said by all the masters . . . . and affords a justly critical, well-digested view of the achievements of each writer of note.'—*The Lady.*

'His **second** work will do much to enhance his reputation as **a critic and thinker** of no mean order.'—*News of the World.*

'**Pleasantly and** intelligently written, and will prove profitable reading.'
Scotsman.

'**Written in a style which at** once fascinates the reader. Each of the men of **genius is presented in a clearly** cut, finely finished literary portrait.'
Sheffield Daily Telegraph.

'Without **a** word of mere verbiage **or** the detestable pretence of fine writing. . . . This book cannot be read without pleasure and instruction.'—*Dublin Evening Mail.*

'Mr. Forster's style is easy and colloquial, and he hits off the salient features of his subjects **very** cleverly.'—*Liverpool Daily Post.*

'These pleasant essays. . . . The author **has** done well to collect them in a more enduring form, of which they are certainly worthy.'—*Cambridge Chronicle.*

'Mr. Forster's sympathetic and sparkling sketches portray the salient characteristics of these famous men in bold relief. An animated style, many anecdotes, and translations of typical passages from their writings, bring the men and their works vividly before the reader.'—*The Bookbuyer, New York.*

'Sincère, vibrant, de lecture amusante, et **très suffisament exact.**'
Le Livre Moderne.

Crown 8vo, vellum cloth, price **6s.**

MIRABILIA VRBIS ROMÆ.

THE MARVELS OF ROME; or, a PICTURE of the GOLDEN CITY.

AN ENGLISH VERSION OF THE MEDIEVAL GUIDE-BOOK,

WITH A SUPPLEMENT OF ILLUSTRATIVE MATTER AND NOTES.

BY FRANCIS MORGAN NICHOLS.

'Mr. Nichols has produced a work which must, as we think, fascinate **all who** are interested in the classical and mediæval antiquities of Rome.'—*Guardian.*

'Many people will be grateful to Mr. Nichols for his very careful English rendering of this curious and interesting little work. The translator's copious notes give the book **a** strong additional interest, and **even** an original value of its own.'—*Scots Observer.*

'Admirably printed, **and bears every mark of competent scholarship.**'—*The Nation (New York).*

4to, with Portrait, ***cloth gilt, price*** **21s.**

THE EARLIEST DOCUMENT RELATING TO AMERICA.

THE LETTER IN SPANISH OF CHRISTOPHER COLUMBUS,

WRITTEN ON HIS RETURN FROM HIS FIRST VOYAGE, AND

ADDRESSED TO LUIS DE SANT ANGEL, 15 FEB.-14 MARCH, 1493,

ANNOUNCING THE DISCOVERY OF THE NEW WORLD.

Reproduced in Facsimile, from a Unique Copy. With Introductory and Critical Remarks, &c., **and** a Literal Translation into English.

'A reprint of absorbing interest.'—*Saturday Review.*

'Messrs. Ellis & Elvey have done a service to the history of maritime discovery by the reproduction in facsimile of Columbus's Letter to Luis de Sant Angel.'—*Athenæum.*

Ellis & Elvey's Publications.

Crown 4to. on hand-made paper, cloth, price £2 2s.

IMPRESSION OF 128 COPIES ONLY.

THE HALL OF LAWFORD HALL.

Records of an Essex House and of its Proprietors from the Saxon Times to the Reign of Henry VIII.

[AN HISTORICAL AND TOPOGRAPHICAL WORK
By FRANCIS MORGAN NICHOLS, F.S.A.]

This volume has grown out of a description (not originally intended for publication) of the hall of a country house containing shields of arms of its ancient proprietors.

Among other matter founded mainly on original research, it includes full biographies of Sir John Say, Under-Treasurer of England and Speaker of the House of Commons in the reign of Henry VI. and Edward IV.; of William, Lord Mountjoy (the friend of Erasmus); and of the Marquess and Marchioness of Exeter of the time of Henry VIII.

It also contains an account of the circumstances attending the death of Humfrey, Duke of Gloucester, with notices, derived from the Public Records, of the distribution of his property in anticipation of, and immediately after, his death.

OPINIONS OF THE PRESS.

'An excellent book. . . . . It contains a most valuable contribution to the history of England from Henry VI. to Henry VIII., and what is practically a very able life, and exhaustive account of the tragical death, of Humphrey, Duke of Gloucester, from original sources. . . . . As a contribution to local history it also deserves the highest praise, for the history of the manor has been written probably more thoroughly than any history of any manor has been written before.'—*Athenæum.*

'To trace the fortunes of an actual house from Saxon times to the reign of Henry VIII. has all the attraction of a novel, especially as it continually brings us into touch with such well-known historical characters as Duke Humphrey and Erasmus, Lord Mountjoy, and others.'—*Globe.*

'The local and county history that are found in these pages make it a volume much to be desired by Essex collectors: whilst the hitherto unpublished particulars relative to the Mountjoys and their Derbyshire estates at Barton-Blount are of value to those interested in the historic or manorial details of the midland shire. . . . . It throws real light on the by-paths of our national history.'—*Antiquary.*

'Mr. Nichols has woven in with the history of Lawford Hall so many valuable and interesting points connected with the history of the country, and he treats his subject in so readable and pleasant a style, that we are inclined to wish either that he had set himself the task of surveying some larger field of history, or that this local work, which possesses so much of general interest, could find its way into the hands of more readers.'—*Essex Standard.*

Eighth Edition, small 8vo, half bound, price 5s.

HUNTING SONGS.

By the late R. E. EGERTON-WARBURTON,
OF ARLEY HALL, CHESHIRE.

---

29 NEW BOND STREET, LONDON, W.

www.ingramcontent.com/pod-product-compliance
Lightning Source LLC
Chambersburg PA
CBHW032122230426
43672CB00009B/1833